Workshop on Natural Language Processing in E-Commerce (EComNLP 2020)

Held online due to COVID-19

Barcelona, Spain
12 December 2020

ISBN: 978-1-7138-2826-6

COLING 2020

The 2020 International Conference on Computational Linguistics

Proceedings of the Workshop on Natural Language Processing in E-Commerce (EComNLP)

December 12, 2020
Barcelona, Spain (Online)

Introduction

Welcome to the Workshop on Natural Language Processing in E-Commerce. We received 22 submissions, and due to a rigorous review process, we accepted 10 of them. We are grateful for the excellent contributions made from all the authors and reviewers.

Natural Language Processing (NLP) plays an irreplaceable role in modern e-commerce applications. The e-commerce setting presents exciting novel research opportunities in NLP space. The goal of our proposed work shop is to bridge the gap between researchers and practitioners to study the unique set of problems in the intersection of NLP and Ecommerce.

Since its early inception, Ecommerce has benefited significantly from research in NLP areas such as sentiment analysis, summarization, query understanding, entity extraction, machine translation etc. These problems have attracted continual attention from NLP researchers, and several high impact papers have been published in key ACL venues. Re cent advances in areas such as dialog systems, ma chine translation, image tagging etc. have already started influencing the industry. In fact, almost all key research areas in NLP have well matching Ecommerce applications.

The Ecommerce domain in turn has also presented researchers with challenging high impact problems. Selected examples include, aspect level sentiment analysis of product reviews, modeling the unique nature of e commerce queries and associated user behavior, improving search query performance through the rich set of user interactions in search logs, extraction of e-commerce entities and relations on novel document formats etc.

We hope all participants find the workshop helpful, either in academic applications or in industry applications. As ecommerce NLP is a relative new field in the literature, we look forward to learn and share with everyone of you.

Organizers:

Huasha Zhao, Microsoft
Parikshit Sondhi, Snap Inc.
Nguyen Bach, Alibaba Group
Sanjika Hewavitharana, eBay Inc.
Yifan He, Alibaba Group
Luo Si, Alibaba Group
Heng Ji, UIUC

Program Committee:

Markus Dreyer, Amazon
Josef van Genabith, German Research Center for AI
Surya Kallamudi, Home Depot
Honglei Liu, Facebook
Thien Huu Nguyen, University of Oregon
Sen Wu, Stanford University
Qiong Zhang, Alibaba
Shahram Khadivi, eBay Inc.
Selcuk Kopru, eBay Inc.
Xianjing Liu, eBay Inc.
Dingxian Wang, eBay Inc.

Invited Speaker:

Fei Huang, Alibaba Group

Table of Contents

E-Commerce Content and Collaborative-based Recommendation using K-Nearest Neighbors and Enriched Weighted Vectors
Bardia Rafieian and Marta R. Costa-jussà 1

Multi-label classification of promotions in digital leaflets using textual and visual information
Roberto Arroyo, David Jiménez-Cabello and Javier Martínez-Cebrián 11

Bilingual Transfer Learning for Online Product Classification
Erik Lehmann, András Simonyi, Lukas Henkel and Jörn Franke 21

Interrupt me Politely: Recommending Products and Services by Joining Human Conversation
Boris Galitsky and Dmitry Ilvovsky 32

Benchmarking Automated Review Response Generation for the Hospitality Domain
Tannon Kew, Michael Amsler and Sarah Ebling 43

On a Chatbot Navigating a User through a Concept-Based Knowledge Model
Boris Galitsky, Dmitry Ilvovsky and Elizaveta Goncharova 53

BERT-based similarity learning for product matching
Janusz Tracz, Piotr Iwo Wójcik, Kalina Jasinska-Kobus, Riccardo Belluzzo, Robert Mroczkowski
and Ireneusz Gawlik 66

Aspect-Similarity-Aware Historical Influence Modeling for Rating Prediction
Ryo Shimura, Shotaro Misawa, Masahiro Sato, Tomoki Taniguchi and Tomoko Ohkuma 76

Distinctive Slogan Generation with Reconstruction
Shotaro Misawa, Yasuhide Miura, Tomoki Taniguchi and Tomoko Ohkuma 87

Conference Program

15:20-15:30 ***Welcome and Opening Remarks***

15:30-16:00 *NLP Technologies and Applications for e-Commerce*
Fei Huang

16:00-16:15 *Aspect-Similarity-Aware Historical Influence Modeling for Rating Prediction*
Ryo Shimura, Shotaro Misawa, Masahiro Sato, Tomoki Taniguchi and Tomoko Ohkuma

16:15-16:30 *Distinctive Slogan Generation with Reconstruction*
Shotaro Misawa, Yasuhide Miura, Tomoki Taniguchi and Tomoko Ohkuma

16:30-16:45 *E-Commerce Content and Collaborative-based Recommendation using K-Nearest Neighbors and Enriched Weighted Vectors*
Bardia Rafieian and Marta R. Costa-jussà

16:45-17:00 *Multi-label classification of promotions in digital leaflets using textual and visual information*
Roberto Arroyo, David Jiménez-Cabello and Javier Martínez-Cebrián

17:00-17:15 *Bilingual Transfer Learning for Online Product Classification*
Erik Lehmann, András Simonyi, Lukas Henkel and Jörn Franke

17:15-17:30 *Interrupt me Politely: Recommending Products and Services by Joining Human Conversation*
Boris Galitsky and Dmitry Ilvovsky

17:30-17:45 *Benchmarking Automated Review Response Generation for the Hospitality Domain*
Tannon Kew, Michael Amsler and Sarah Ebling

17:45-18:00 *On a Chatbot Navigating a User through a Concept-Based Knowledge Model*
Boris Galitsky, Dmitry Ilvovsky and Elizaveta Goncharova

18:00-18:15 *BERT-based similarity learning for product matching*
Janusz Tracz, Piotr Iwo Wójcik, Kalina Jasinska-Kobus, Riccardo Belluzzo, Robert Mroczkowski and Ireneusz Gawlik

18:15-18:30 *Blending Search and Discovery: Tag-Based Query Refinement with Contextual Reinforcement Learning*
Bingqing Yu and Jacopo Tagliabue

E-Commerce Content and Collaborative-based Recommendation using K-Nearest Neighbors and Enriched Weighted Vectors

Bardia Rafieian*   Marta R. Costa-jussà
TALP Research Center, Universitat Politècnica de Catalunya, Barcelona
{bardia.rafieian,marta.ruiz}@upc.edu

Abstract

In this paper, we present two productive and functional recommender methods to improve the accuracy of predicting the right product for the user. One proposal is a survey-based recommender system that uses k-nearest neighbors. It recommends products by asking questions from the user, efficiently applying a binary product vector to the product attributes, and processing the request with a minimum error. The second proposal uses an enriched collaborative-based recommender system using enriched weighted vectors. Thanks to the style rules, the enriched collaborative-based method recommends outfits with competitive recommendation quality. We evaluated both of the proposals on a Kaggle fashion-dataset along with iMaterialist and, results show equivalent performance on binary gender and product attributes.

1   Introduction

The demanding market of the fashion industry has led to a challenging environment for recommender systems (Nenni et al., 2013). To say, increasing information in the fashion shopping brings confusion to users who have to select the right choice among a huge number of available fashion products. Furthermore, to satisfy the excessive desire of users in the fashion industry, recommendation engines are playing an important role by automating the product selection procedure (Luce, 2018).

A recommender system targets to predict user's tastes and recommend product items that exceptionally are interesting for them. In recommendation engines, the product and the user information is gathered to predict the score or choice of a user to a product. The information collected from a user is either directly or indirectly while the data for products is collected explicitly. In content-based filtering recommendations (Schafer et al., 2007), we explicitly gather information for both users and products and then compare the similarity to recommend the best choice. On the other hand, the collaborative-based algorithm (Bhagavatula et al., 2018) uses "User Behavior" for recommending items. They explore the behavior of users and products in terms of rating, selection, purchase history, and cookies (Isinkaye et al., 2015).

We introduce two settings of recommendation systems for the fashion industry using both types of collaborative and content-based filtering. In the first approach, we propose a survey content-based recommender system and as a second, we introduce an enriched collaborative-based recommender using a novel weighted system. Finally, we initiate style rules that bring simplicity in selecting outfits based on available products.

The rest of the paper is organized as follows. The next section covers an overview of available approaches in fashion recommending systems. Section 3 describes our proposed methods in detail. Section 4 shows the experimental framework and results and finally, section 5 discusses the conclusions and future work of the proposed system.

Proceedings of the Workshop on Natural Language Processing in E-Commerce (EComNLP), pages 1–10
Barcelona, Spain (Online), Dec 12, 2020.

2   Related Works

The wide fashion domain requires studies in the research area to assist the shopping experience. For a long time, the limitation on computing resources was a drawback for companies to apply deep learning algorithms on their platform. Fortunately, now technology allows processing a vast amount of data in a short time. The machine learning field is impacting the fashion industry in several ways including Apparel designing, Manufacturing process and, Virtual merchandising [1]. Several fashion retailers are using question Answering systems (Santoro et al., 2017), Visual search, and automatic product tagging (Hiriyannaiah et al., 2020). Nowadays, NLP as a machine learning technology improves the field of personalization by extracting the product characteristics such as attributes, reviews, feedback, and other information [2].

Recently, the fashion industry is developing outfit recommenders by using machine learning techniques to decrease the time for exploring and combining products along with trended styles.

Consequently, in (Lin et al., 2018) they addressed the task of outfit recommendation by suggesting a bag of lower body clothes to a selected top. That is to say, a neural multi-task learning framework, called neural outfit recommendation (NOR) has been introduced consisting of two: a convolutional neural network with an attention mechanism to mine visual attributes of products and then a recurrent neural network to translate the visual information into text format. As a result, the mutual information among products is discovered and the system can recommend outfits using these features.

In (Akshaya et al., 2018) they used K-Nearest Neighbour algorithm to detect the nearest neighbor or a cluster based on the k value. There is also a considerable amount of work on recommending different types of categories such as dresses, backbags, heels and handbags along with rating top k products to display (Li et al., 2010). One implemented solution uses a text mining approach to improve ranked based recommender systems. Also, in (Ahuja et al., 2019) a combination of k-means Clustering (Singh et al., 2020) (Jin and Han, 2010) along with k-Nearest Neighbor is implemented on the movielens dataset (Harper and Konstan, 2015) to achieve an improving result. In their proposed technique, the recommender system predicts the user's preference for a movie based on different parameters which also can be applied to product categories in the fashion industry.

3   Proposed Methods

This section describes the two proposed methods of our recommender system. The first subsection explains the survey content-based recommender system architecture within an example. The second subsection provides the enriched collaborative-based recommender system with the stylist, including architecture and examples.

3.1   Survey content-based recommender system

In a survey content-based recommender systems, we rely on replies to product survey questions and try to locate the most similar products. To address this, we require a dataset of product vectors and a replied-on-survey vector with the same dimension as the product vectors. The product dataset includes product information in the form of binary vectors. Table 1 shows an example of the database format of the product table. In this example, there are two different classes each has three sub-classes for totally three products:

Product_id	Class1	Class2
Product_1	Subclass1	Subclass1
Product_2	Subclass2	Subclass2
Product_3	Subclass3	Subclass3

Table 1: Database format of the product table.

---

[1] https://medium.com/datadriveninvestor/
[2] https://www.information-age.com/natural-language-processing-explained-123480247/

To prepare the data for training, we created a binary table from the original one, including only 0 and 1 values. As a result, we extended columns to classes.sub-classes values. Table 2 shows the transformed format of the original table 1.

Product_id	Class1.Sub1	Class1.Sub2	Class1.Subc3	Class2.Sub1	Class2.Sub2	Class2.Sub3
Product_1	0/1	0/1	0/1	0/1	0/1	0/1
Product_2	0/1	0/1	0/1	0/1	0/1	0/1
Product_3	0/1	0/1	0/1	0/1	0/1	0/1

Table 2: Modified database format of product table.

Let's consider $\vec{P_i}$ as product vectors and $\vec{R}$ as a reply vector. As a first step, we train unsupervised K-Nearest Neighbors (Knn) (Peterson, 2009) on all $\vec{P_i} = \{ \vec{P_1}, \dots ,\vec{P_n}\}$ vectors using Euclidean distance so that for each $\vec{P_i}$ the distance is calculated. At this step, we train all categories of products. Considering $\vec{P_1}$ and $\vec{P_2}$ as two sample vectors, the distance D is calculated as shown in equation 1.

$$D(\vec{P_1}, \vec{P_2}) = ||\vec{P_1} - \vec{P_2}|| = \sqrt[2]{(\vec{P_{1_1}} - \vec{P_{2_1}})^2 + (\vec{P_{1_2}} - \vec{P_{2_2}})^2 + \dots + (\vec{P_{1_n}} - \vec{P_{2_n}})^2} \qquad (1)$$

Afterward, through a survey, we receive information and create a reply vector equivalent to the product vector in terms of size. More precisely, in the survey, there are questions for each sub-class equivalent to the product classes. Then, at each session, the user selects the required sub-class in each class. Finally, for each reply, recommendations are chosen from its n best predictions. The n number of predicted recommendations can be defined or modified at each training by the e-commerce platform manager.

3.2 Enriched collaborative-based recommender system

The enriched collaborative-based recommender system pretends to take advantage of extra user external information. Traditional collaborative-based recommender systems reply to users' historical preferences on a set of items. Because they are based on historical data, the main assumption is users who have agreed in the past items to also agree in the future ones (Schafer et al., 2007). we propose to inject: the history of clicks and feedback, the clicked product and, styles.

3.2.1 Injected information

History of clicks: We require the set of past clicked products by each user to track their preference, as shown in equation 2.

$$\vec{C} = \{\vec{C_i}|\vec{C_i} \in \vec{P}, and\langle c, c\rangle = \langle p, p\rangle\} \qquad (2)$$

where $\vec{C}$ is the set of clicked products and $\vec{P}$ is the vector of products. Then, we sum up all vectors in $\vec{C_i}$ as $\vec{SC}$ by considering n as a number of product vectors in the history of clicks, as shown in equation 3.

$$SC = \sum_{i=1}^{n} \vec{C_i} \qquad (3)$$

where $\vec{SC}$ includes sum of all vector elements. Then, executing the algorithm 1, we select maximum values in all elements of $\vec{SC}$ as 1 and the rest as 0.

Result: Return SC
for *element in SC* **do**
    if *element is Maximum* **then**
        element = 1;
    else
        element = 0;
    end
end

Algorithm 1: Creating a binary vector from maximum values of the history of clicks

History of feedback (rating): We assume each user is able to rate each product by its own preference as shown in equation 4.

$$F_{p_x} = \begin{cases} 1, & \text{like} \\ 0, & \text{not rated} \\ -1, & \text{dislike} \end{cases} \tag{4}$$

where F_{p_x} is feedback on product P_i by user X_i. Further, we discuss in detail the way we use this data.

Clicked product: The clicked product (CP) returns the corresponded vector of the product so that we use it to find similar products into our trained model. At this step, we already have trained models varied by main product categories. Next, n number of similar products to the clicked one is detected by Euclidean distance.

Styles: Styles are predefined patterns to combine products as an outfit. To say, each style includes several clothes with predefined category, subcategory and, color. We have styles that ranged from two to five products to complete any outfit. Table 3 gives a sample of style including three products with predefined attributes which complete an outfit. Table 3 gives a sample of style including three products with predefined attributes which complete an outfit.

{ "Product1":[{ "Category":"Dress", "Subcategory":"Nightdress", "Color":"Blue" }]
,"Product2": [{ "Category":"Footwear", "Subcategory":"Sandals", "Color":"Black"}]
"Product3":[{ "Category":"Accessory", "Subcategory":"Belt", "Color":"Black" }]}

Table 3: Sample of style including 3 products with predefined attributes.

After retrieving a bag of similar products to the clicked one, we look for the best style to create an outfit.

3.2.2 Method to inject information

In the next, we explain how the communication between injected parts is done. The proposed system works using three main steps to recommend an outfit to a specific user.

Step1 : In this step, the product information is taken as input and we create the new data by transforming the raw data into a binary matrix. In tables 4 and 5 we illustrate a real example of normal and transformed matrix table of products respectively.

Product_id	Cat	Subcat	Color
Product_1	shirt	tshirt	red
Product_2	dress	blazer	black
Product_3	footwear	sanadals	white
Product_4	pants	boots	black
Product_5	shirt	boots	white

Table 4: A normal form of the product table

Product_id	Cat.Shirt	Cat.Dress	Cat.Footwear	Cat.Pants	Subcat.Tshirt	...	Color.Red	Color.Black	Color.white
Product_1	0/1	0/1	0/1	0/1	0/1		0/1	0/1	0/1
Product_2	0/1	0/1	0/1	0/1	0/1		0/1	0/1	0/1
Product_3	0/1	0/1	0/1	0/1	0/1		0/1	0/1	0/1
Product_4	0/1	0/1	0/1	0/1	0/1		0/1	0/1	0/1
Product_5	0/1	0/1	0/1	0/1	0/1		0/1	0/1	0/1

Table 5: A transformed form of the product table 4

Then, a history of feedback for each user is stored in the database by each feedback (like or dislike). As mentioned, a product can be rated by each user so that its user based to respect the other user's feedback. In the initial point, when there is no feedback, we select all of the products to perform similarity detection, but once we reach a considerable amount of feedback on a product, we select 80% of liked and 20% of unrated products to recommend. The disliked products are ignored and marked as a blacklist in the database. using user-based feedback, we ensure disliked products are still available for other users. Later, the history of clicks is another input stored in the database to keep a track of user preferences. By using this information, we give a higher weight to the features in which the user has a higher interest. As an example, user a has clicked more on products with black color and leather material, so we try to recommend products including these features. However, these features are being changed during the lifetime of a user in the system so that their preferences are dynamic for different categories. For instance, the recommended color will change once the weight of the current color is less than the previous one due to the clicks on the other type of colors. Afterward, the styles are injected into the database to combine recommended products as outfits. we started with 1000 style patterns with the mentioned format. In the discussion part, we explain the future available tasks for this part. And finally, once a user clicks on a product, we keep the vector of this product as a temporary value to detect its similar products. The important point at this step is the way we store the product information. That is, in order to prevent recommending the same category (for example, recommending always shirt to a clicked shirt product), we store products by different categories and detect similar products in different categories. In the next step, we explain the algorithm we used.

Step 2: After storing the recommended information, we follow Algorithm 2 procedure to prepare the recommended products. Considering k as a number of required products in each category, CP as a current clicked product by the user, P_c as a list of products divided by categories(c), SC as a binary list of history of clicks and F as a list of user's feedback.

Result: $Return Recommended List (recommended products by category)$
initialization;
$input(k)$;
$open(P_c)$;
$open(SC)$;
$open(F)$;
$open(CP)$;
for $(category in P_c)$ **do**
    for $product in category$ **do**
        if $((F_p == 1) and (SC is in product))$ **then**
            $ListLiked = add(product)$;
        end
        if $((F_p == 0) and (SC is in product))$ **then**
            $ListUnrated = add(product)$;
        end
    end
    $Trainset = 80\%(k)(ListLiked) + 20\%(k)(ListUnrated)$;
    $RecommendedList = insert(K nearest neighbors(Trainset))$;
end

Algorithm 2: Creating a list of the recommended products per category

Step3: Having the list of recommended products we try to fit products in style rules. We look for a match between recommended products in styles in terms of $Category$, $Subcategory$ and $Color$, as soon as a match is found, we return that list as a total look. Algorithm 3 describes the approach we produce outfit out of recommended products. Table 6 shows an example of a recommended outfit including four products:

{"Product133":[{ "Category":"tops", "Subcategory":"formaltop", "Color":"red" "Fabrics:"Cotton" }]
"Product87": [{ "Category":"Footwear", "Subcategory":"boot", "Color":"Blue", "Fabrics:"Foam" }]
"Product91": [{ "Category":"pants", "Subcategory":"jeans", "Color":"Blue", "Fabrics:"Denim" }]}

Table 6: Example of recommended outfit.

```
Result: A list of clothes as outfit
initialization;
open(Styles);
open(RecommendedList);
for style in Styles do
    if (RecommendedList is in style) then
        Return list of products;
    end
end
```

Algorithm 3: Creating outfit out of recommended products with Style rules

4   Experiments

Data   We perform our experiment on Kaggle fashion-dataset[3] along with iMaterialist[4] with totally around 90k rows and 8 columns. The information of each of the columns included gender, master category, subcategory, article type, base color, year, season, and usage. In total, there are 15 product categories: accessories, bag, beachwear, coats, hat, hosiery, footwear, apparel set, bottom wear, dress, innerwear, loungewear, saree, socks, and topwear. This is a gender-balanced dataset (considering binary classification), we have approximately 48% women and 52% men proportion entries. We are aware of the limitation of the binarization in gender, where other communities from LGTB+ are disregarded, unfortunately non-binary gender is not currently included in this data.

Data Privacy   We undertake to comply with the legislation in force regarding the protection of personal data contained in the RGPD 2016/679 UE. The basis for legitimizing the processing of the data is the consent of the interested party. We carry out the treatments related to the scope of the consent and informed purposes. The data provided will be kept for the duration of the contractual relationship and during the years necessary to comply with legal obligations. The data will not be transferred to third parties, except for group companies. We perform the recommender on the data provided by the business to business partners with all of the privacy respects and regulations accepted by them and their final users.

Survey content-based recommender system results   In our first experiment we evaluated our survey content-based recommender described in Section 3.1 with 1,000 random answered surveys. Then, we compared the results by Root Mean Square Error (RMSE) based on equation 5.

$$MSE = \frac{1}{n} \sum_{i=1}^{n} (Y_i - Y_i')^2 \tag{5}$$

We compared the MSE between requested and queried products when assigning k number of nearest neighbors to the surveyed product. Figure 1 shows the MSE difference for two settings with $k = 5$ and $k = 10$.

---

[3]https://www.kaggle.com/paramaggarwal/fashion-product-images-dataset?
[4]https://www.kaggle.com/c/imaterialist-fashion-2019-FGVC6/data?select=train

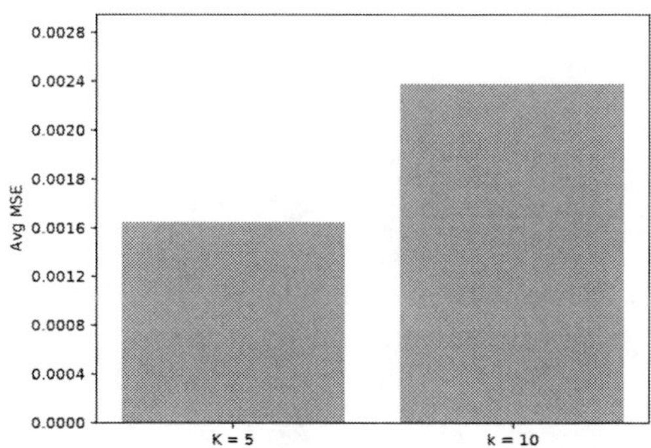

Figure 1: Mean square error for 1,000 surveys on 90k data in two settings: $k = 5$ and $k = 10$

To visualize results, we provided five random surveys (expected) and its 5 nearest neighbors found with knn recommender system from section 3.1. We selected random products as input with related vector and performed the experiment. Figure 2 illustrates the expected products in the first row and the recommended ones in the rest in five different requests per column. We can see the category and other attributes in the recommendations are close to the expected product.

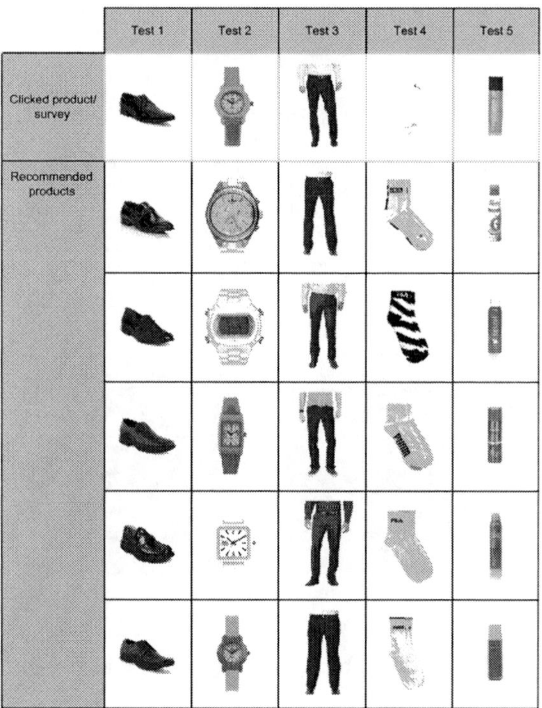

Figure 2: A visualization of k = 5 recommended products for random requests

Collaborative-based recommender system results. We evaluated our second recommender system explained in the section 3.2. In this experiment, we grouped the dataset by product categories such that we find similar products to each clicked-product in different product catalogs. To perform our analysis, totally we created 8 categories out of 10 available in the dataset. Next, the proposed approach performed on the clicked-product and outfits was achieved by using our pre-defined style patterns. We selected five random output samples from the proposed recommender in figure 3.

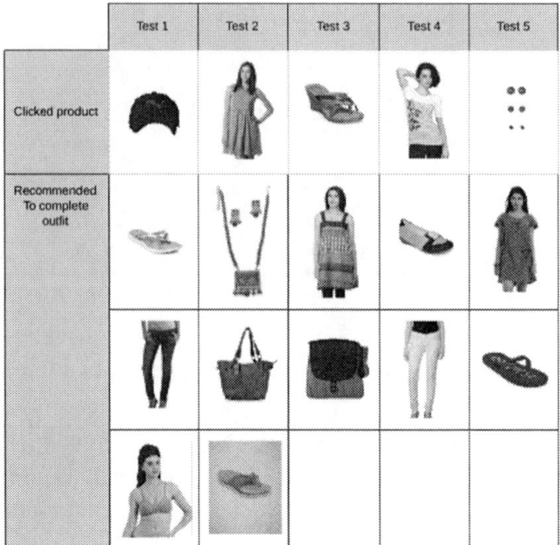

Figure 3: A visualization of full outfit recommendations for the clicked-product using the style rules for five random cases

As shown in Figure 4, the average MSE has decreased by 4.5%, which is a significant decrease in the error.

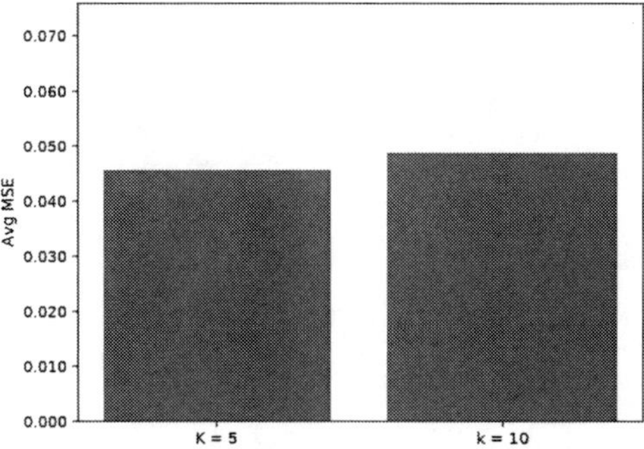

Figure 4: Average MSE in the Collaborative-based recommender in two different settings

Gender analysis. In our setting, once a user clicks on a product should get some recommendations. The system is not aware of any information about the gender of this person and there is no gender filter on products. We want to evaluate the performance of our system desegregated by gender. Referring to the details in 5, we achieved more than 99% accuracy in recommending the product to the correct gender. The results indicated on the bar chart shows similar performance on men-women which is due to a balanced dataset. Moreover, we have improved the gender selection by up to 100% by giving a higher weight to the gender vectors in the clicked product.

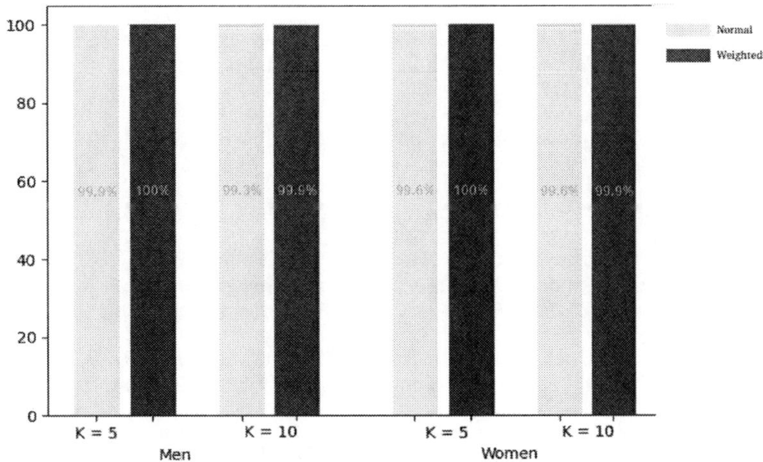

Figure 5: Results of recommending the correct product gender to men and women in normal and weighted modes of vectors

5   Conclusions

Recommender systems are becoming one of the main key points in e-commerce and today customers are demanding more personalized products. In our approach, two recommender systems were introduced where each one has specific usage in the e-commerce platform. The survey content-based recommender system suggests the nearest product based on the replies on the survey with the least distance. On the other hand, the enriched collaborative-based recommender system uses more filters and style rules to create outfits based on the clicked product with similar performance on a gender basis (assuming binary gender). However, there are remaining challenges in updating style rules or missing some products in case of using a few numbers of neighbors. As future work, we plan to develop an enriched collaborative-based recommender system by using more external information and dynamically updating styles based on the local trends.

Acknowledgments

We thank the anonymous reviewers for their insightful comments. This work is supported in part by the Viume Company through research and development of the online e-commerce platform and by the Spanish Ministerio de Ciencia e Innovación and the Agencia Estatal de Investigación, through the postdoctoral senior grant Ramón y Cajal.

References

Rishabh Ahuja, Arun Solanki, and Anand Nayyar. 2019. Movie recommender system using k-means clustering and k-nearest neighbor. pages 263–268, 01.

Srikanth Akshaya, Parvaneh Kamali, and P.Sudha. 2018. Outfit recommender system using knn algorithm. *International journal of engineering research and technology*, 6.

Chandra Bhagavatula, Sergey Feldman, Russell Power, and Waleed Ammar. 2018. Content-based citation recommendation. In *Proceedings of the 2018 Conference of the North American Chapter of the Association for Computational Linguistics: Human Language Technologies, Volume 1 (Long Papers)*, Louisiana, June.

F. Maxwell Harper and Joseph A. Konstan. 2015. The movielens datasets: History and context. *ACM Transactions on Interactive Intelligent Systems*, 5(4), December.

Srinidhi Hiriyannaiah, Siddesh G M, and K. Srinivasa. 2020. Deep visual ensemble similarity (dvesm) approach for visually aware recommendation and search in smart community. *Journal of King Saud University - Computer and Information Sciences*, 04.

Folasade Olubusola Isinkaye, Yetunde Folajimi, and Bolanle Adefowoke Ojokoh. 2015. Recommendation systems: Principles, methods and evaluation. *Egyptian Informatics Journal*, 16:261–273.

Xin Jin and Jiawei Han, 2010. *K-Means Clustering*, pages 563–564. Springer US, Boston, MA.

Yize Li, Jiazhong Nie, Yi Zhang, Bingqing Wang, Baoshi Yan, and Fuliang Weng. 2010. Contextual recommendation based on text mining. In *Proceedings of the 23rd International Conference on Computational Linguistics: Posters*, COLING '10, page 692–700, USA. Association for Computational Linguistics.

Yujie Lin, Pengjie Ren, Zhumin Chen, Zhaochun Ren, Jun Ma, and Maarten de Rijke. 2018. Explainable fashion recommendation with joint outfit matching and comment generation. *CoRR*, abs/1806.08977.

Leanne Luce. 2018. *Artificial Intelligence for Fashion: How AI is Revolutionizing the Fashion Industry*. Apress.

Maria Elena Nenni, Luca Giustiniano, and Luca Pirolo. 2013. Demand forecasting in the fashion industry: A review. *International Journal of Engineering Business Management*, 5.

L. E. Peterson. 2009. K-nearest neighbor. *Scholarpedia*, 4(2):1883. revision #137311.

Adam Santoro, David Raposo, David G. T. Barrett, Mateusz Malinowski, Razvan Pascanu, Peter W. Battaglia, and Timothy P. Lillicrap. 2017. A simple neural network module for relational reasoning. *CoRR*, abs/1706.01427.

J. Ben Schafer, Dan Frankowski, Jon Herlocker, and Shilad Sen, 2007. *Collaborative Filtering Recommender Systems*, pages 291–324. Springer Berlin Heidelberg, Berlin, Heidelberg.

Tarana Singh, Anand Nayyar, and Arun Solanki. 2020. Multilingual opinion mining movie recommendation system using rnn. In Pradeep Kumar Singh, Wiesław Pawłowski, Sudeep Tanwar, Neeraj Kumar, Joel J. P. C. Rodrigues, and Mohammad Salameh Obaidat, editors, *Proceedings of First International Conference on Computing, Communications, and Cyber-Security (IC4S 2019)*, pages 589–605, Singapore. Springer Singapore.

Multi-label classification of promotions in digital leaflets using textual and visual information

Roberto Arroyo, David Jiménez-Cabello and Javier Martínez-Cebrián

Nielsen Connect R&D AI

Calle Salvador de Madariaga, 1, 28027, Madrid, Spain

https://www.nielsen.com/

{roberto.arroyo, david.jimenez, javier.martinezcebrian}@nielsen.com

Abstract

Product descriptions in e-commerce platforms contain detailed and valuable information about retailers assortment. In particular, coding promotions within digital leaflets are of great interest in e-commerce as they capture the attention of consumers by showing regular promotions for different products. However, this information is embedded into images, making it difficult to extract and process for downstream tasks. In this paper, we present an end-to-end approach that classifies promotions within digital leaflets into their corresponding product categories using both visual and textual information. Our approach can be divided into three key components: 1) region detection, 2) text recognition and 3) text classification. In many cases, a single promotion refers to multiple product categories, so we introduce a multi-label objective in the classification head. We demonstrate the effectiveness of our approach for two separated tasks: 1) image-based detection of the descriptions for each individual promotion and 2) multi-label classification of the product categories using the text from the product descriptions. We train and evaluate our models using a private dataset composed of images from digital leaflets obtained by Nielsen. Results show that we consistently outperform the proposed baseline by a large margin in all the experiments.

1 Introduction

The latest advances in Artificial Intelligence (AI) have provided new tools to enhance the automation of different recognition problems. We are witnessing a clear trend to merge different domains within AI to obtain better representations for the most complex problems. Many recent approaches merge textual and visual information by applying Natural Language Processing (NLP) and Computer Vision (CV), with the aim of solving problems that involve both text and images (Bai et al., 2018). Within this context, structured knowledge extraction from unstructured text is an open problem in the e-commerce literature (Arroyo et al., 2019). Regardless the source of the information (*e.g.* product websites, product images captured from stores or digital leaflets), it refers to a unified concept that can be denoted as "automated product coding", *i.e.* the extraction of attribute values of e-commerce products (see Fig. 1).

Our present work focuses on the case of knowledge extraction from digital leaflets. Most retailers are replacing physical leaflets, that are directly collected from the stores, with digital leaflets that are uploaded in the cloud on the retailers websites. Comparing to real-world e-commerce platforms that contain billions of products with detailed descriptions (including ratings and opinions), digital leaflets include concise textual and visual information of promotions that applies to some of the products of the store assortment for a short period of time and thus it has to be updated regularly. The knowledge extraction of digital leaflets is of great interest for the e-commerce business as it impacts not only on several aspects of the consumers behaviour or seasonality, but also modifies relevant attributes of the products periodically, *e.g.* price or volume.

In this paper, we bring for the first time the problem of automated product coding in digital leaflets for e-commerce. In particular, we present an approach to predict the product categories for each of the promotions within the leaflet that serves as a strong baseline for future works. Technically, this is

Proceedings of the Workshop on Natural Language Processing in E-Commerce (EComNLP), pages 11–20

Barcelona, Spain (Online), Dec 12, 2020.

| (a) Region-based detection. | (b) Text recognition and extraction. | (c) Multi-label text classification. |

Figure 1: Key components of our approach for a single promotion within a digital leaflet.

a multi-label text classification problem as some promotions can potentially apply to several product categories. For that purpose, we hypothesize that most of the information of the promotions is self-contained in the products descriptions, so we first detect all these regions within the image that contain textual descriptions and extract the text using Optical Character Recognition (OCR) techniques. In Fig. 1, we show a visual representation of the three key components in the proposed approach: 1) region-based detection of the promotions description, 2) text recognition and extraction, and 3) multi-label text classification.

The building blocks depicted in Fig. 1 also relate to the different domains covered in the approach and they can be divided into the following three categories: 1) **CV**: a region detection architecture based on deep learning and image processing to detect the descriptions of each individual promotion within the digital leaflet, 2) **CV+NLP**: a text recognition method for extracting the textual information contained into the detected descriptions based on OCR and 3) **NLP**: a multi-label text classification model based on sub-word text embeddings and a shallow neural network.

The main contributions of the paper are three fold:

1. We bring for the first time the problem of automated item coding in digital leaflets for e-commerce platforms.

2. We formulate the process for predicting the categorization of each individual promotion within digital leaflets as a multi-label classification problem, which uses both CV and NLP techniques for properly fusing image and text information.

3. We conduct several experiments to assess the performance of the model for several aspects: a) detection of the product description region in promotions, b) multi-label classification of the product categories and c) multi-lingual capabilities.

The contents of the paper are structured as follows: related works are described in Section 2. The technical proposal presented in this paper is described in Section 3. The data used in the evaluations of our proposal, the experiments carried out to validate it and several comparative results are reviewed in Section 4. The final conclusions derived from this paper are discussed in Section 5.

2 Related Work

Prior works related to the fusion of NLP and CV have experienced an important growth in the last years due to the advances in deep learning and its influence in both domains. It covers several fields such as text retrieval (Gomez et al., 2018), image detection and classification (Bai et al., 2018) or automated item coding (Arroyo et al., 2019).

Regarding the first step of the system proposed in this paper, approaches based on region detection over images have received an incredible attention in the last few years. The popularization of deep learning jointly with Convolutional Neural Networks (CNN) (Krizhevsky et al., 2012) has completely changed the traditional paradigm in CV. Standard CNNs are commonly applied only for image classification. However, R-CNNs (R stands for Region-based) are focused on object detection, which combines both detection and classification. Nowadays, techniques such as Faster R-CNN (Ren et al., 2015) are broadly extended to localize and classify objects over images. In this method, the regions in the R-CNN are detected by a selective search algorithm based on a Region Proposal Network (RPN). YOLO (Redmon et al., 2016) is also a technique very popularized for object detection which is focused on Single Shot Detection (SSD) (Liu et al., 2016). Similar proposals based on R-CNN architectures can be used in our approach to initially detect the regions where the text of the leaflets descriptions is located over the images.

Following with the second stage for the recognition of the texts contained in descriptions regions, Optical Character recognition (OCR) is a broad topic covered in the AI community and it aims at extracting text from images, thus working in the intersection between CV and NLP. The most recent approaches use deep learning techniques (Lee and Osindero, 2016) to examine images pixel by pixel, looking for shapes that match the character traits. Available OCR engines comprise implemented solutions that are open-source and proprietary. Calamari (Wick et al., 2020) or Tesseract (Zacharias et al., 2020) are some of the most effective open-source approaches, with lots of users around the world. However, proprietary solutions such as Google OCR[1] are currently obtaining better results in text recognition, including support for a larger number of languages. Our goal is to apply OCR-based algorithms over the regions previously detected using a R-CNN architecture in order to obtain the product descriptions over the images of leaflets.

In the final stage of our described approach, the textual information extracted from the detected regions is classified into their corresponding product categories. The state of the art in short text classification is recently moving to approaches based on DNNs (Deep Neural Networks). On the one hand, in (Joulin et al., 2017) the authors proposed to incorporate sub-word level information to train textual embeddings very efficiently for text classification. On the other hand, the BERT architecture described in (Devlin et al., 2018) also supposed a great milestone in natural language modeling introducing a self-supervised learning strategy that is able to incorporate an architecture based on Transformers (Vaswani et al., 2017) leveraging a large corpus for training. The embeddings obtained using BERT approaches highly correlate with the linguistic context within a sentence. Thus, proposals based on sub-word level information are very competitive compared to BERT models on those cases where we have unstructured textual information and probably OCR errors, such as the descriptions processed in most of the leaflets. It must be also noted that although BERT is focused on standard text processing, there are derived approaches that are also diving into text processing associated with images, such as ViLBERT (Lu et al., 2019) or VL-BERT (Su et al., 2020). The difference is that these recent approaches are not directly applied to classification over text contained in images, they are used for tasks that involve images and related external text, such as VQA (Visual Question Answering) (Antol et al., 2015).

3 Our Proposal for Digital Leaflets Categorization

The leaflets categorization proposal presented in this paper is focused on the prediction of multiple product categories from images such as the depicted in Fig. 1, which is showing a part of a catalog representing specific products. The solution can be divided into the following three main parts:

1. Detection of the regions related to the textual descriptions of each product in a promotion.

2. Recognition of the associated text inside the regions of the detected descriptions.

3. Classification of the recognized text into the different product categories of interest.

In this section, we introduce these three main components of the proposed approach, jointly with the whole leaflets categorization pipeline that combines them to obtain the final output.

---

[1] https://cloud.google.com/vision/docs/ocr

3.1 Region-based Detection

The method designed for detecting the regions that contain the texts associated with product descriptions is based on an R-CNN schema, as presented in Fig 2. We decided to use this CV approach because the texts of product descriptions over the images have a specific appearance format that can be effectively visually differentiated, even when several templates and styles are used for varied retailers. Then, the texts from descriptions can be effectively separated from the rest of the texts in the image.

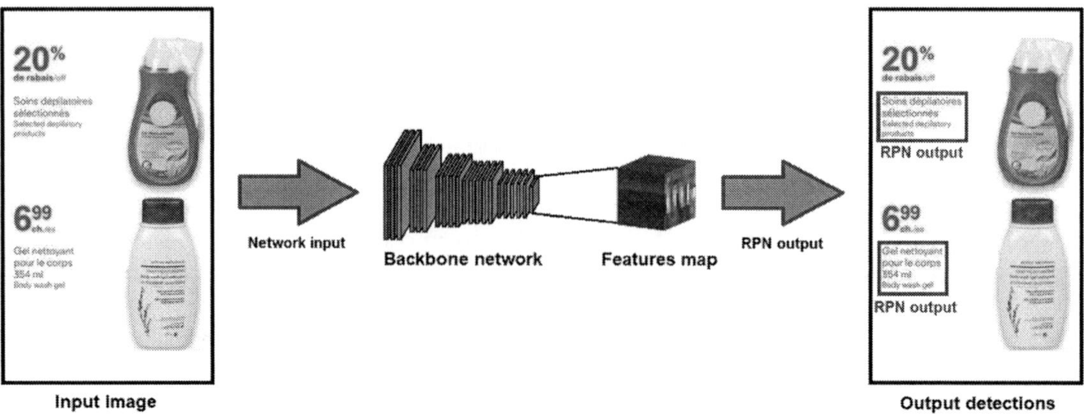

Figure 2: Visual representation of the text region detection over images in our R-CNN architecture.

Initially, we tried to differentiate the product descriptions from the rest of the texts in the digital leaflets by only considering predictions with high confidence in the multi-label text classification proposed for the third part of the system (described in detail in Section 3.3). Unfortunately, a great amount of texts out of scope were classified with high confidences by the model, so we decided to design the approach based on the R-CNN architecture to obtain more accurate results in the overall process.

As can be seen in Fig. 2, our architecture applies an internal Region Proposal Network (RPN) (Ren et al., 2015) with the aim of detecting the positions of the regions of interest. First of all, the image is resized before feeding it into the backbone CNN. This resizing is important to have similar detection schemas independently of the different sizes that could have the input images. For every point in the output, the network has to learn whether a text description region is present in the image at its corresponding position and estimate its size. Several anchors over the input image are used for each location from the backbone network. These anchors indicate possible objects in various sizes and aspect ratios at this location. As the RPN walks through each pixel in the feature map, it has to validate whether these corresponding anchors spanning the input image contain regions of interest. Besides, it has to refine the coordinates of anchors to provide bounding boxes as proposed regions associated with the different text of products descriptions. In order to help with this process, Non-Maximum Suppression (NMS) (Rothe et al., 2014) is applied as follows:

1. Choose the bounding box that has the highest confidence score.

2. Compute its overlap with the rest of bounding boxes and remove the bounding boxes that overlap more than an Intersection over Union (IoU) (Rezatofighi et al., 2019) threshold.

3. Return to the first step and iterate until there are no more boxes with a lower confidence score than the chosen box.

In order to train the detection model, our architecture requires Ground-Truth (GT) information about bounding boxes from sample images, with the aim of training the network to localize the regions of interest. In standard R-CNN architectures, a part of the network is in charge of classifying the bounding boxes into several classes. However, in our schema this is not required, because we do not need to differentiate the class of the bounding boxes detected, what we need is to classify the internal textual information in the stage of text classification that is detailed in Section 3.3. Then, the standard network part for classifying the obtained visual embeddings is not applied in our model, only the part for localization based on RPN previously explained.

3.2 Text Recognition and Extraction

A method based on OCR is used in this second stage in order to recognize the text associated with the previously detected product descriptions. We use Google OCR as basis of our text recognition pipeline. Besides, the goal of our work is not focused on contributing a new complete OCR engine, which is a research out of the scope of this paper that considers a full detection, recognition and classification schema for leaflets categorization.

In our case, OCR converts leaflets images into machine-readable text data. The human visual system reads text by recognizing the patterns of light and dark, translating those patterns into characters and words, and then attaching meaning to it. Similarly, OCR attempts to mimic our visual system by using neural networks.

The approach applied in this stage to compute OCR returns the characters, words and paragraphs obtained from images and their locations. Initially, we implemented the idea of directly clustering the words recognized inside a bounding box detected for a product description, with the aim of providing the whole text string associated with that specific product description. However, we observed that the resulting text string sometimes contained errors due to other out-of-scope texts around the text of interest that interfere with it. To minimize the impact of this recognition issue, we decided to apply a mask to blacken all the parts of the image that are not contained inside the bounding boxes detected in the previous stage by the region detection model. Then, the blackened regions do not interfere with the regions of interest related to product descriptions during the OCR computation. The described blackened process is exemplified in Fig. 1 (b).

Finally, the text extracted by the OCR is post-processed to reduce typical errors, such as the ones associated with strange symbols incorrectly detected, problems derived from lower and upper case letters or dictionary-based corrections.

3.3 Multi-label Text Classification

After recognizing the text corresponding to product descriptions in digital leaflets images, a text classification model is applied to predict the different product categories of interest. Each product can be associated with more than one category, so this use case can be considered as an instance multi-label classification problem.

The proposed text classification model is based on FastText (Joulin et al., 2017), as it efficiently scales in the number of categories to predict. The defined architecture is a simple neural network that contains only one layer. The architecture generates a bag-of-words representation of the text, where the embeddings are fetched for every single word. After that, the embeddings are averaged to obtain a single embedding for the whole text in the hidden layer. Once the averaged embeddings are computed, the single vector is fed to independent binary classifiers for each label (one-vs-all loss). Character n-grams are used, which are really beneficial for text classification problems based on product descriptions (not natural language as it is usually known) and that may also include typos from the OCR. In order to visually understand the architecture and n-grams computation, Fig. 3 is presented.

For training the text classification model, a dataset with manually labeled annotations about the categories associated with each text description is required, as explained in detail in Section 4.1. The trained model is used to perform the inference of the categories related to each promotion description. The inference output gives a vector with probabilities for each available category. A threshold is used to filter the categories corresponding to an instance based on the obtained probabilities, with the aim of providing the multi-label classification. The categories with probabilities above this threshold are considered as positive.

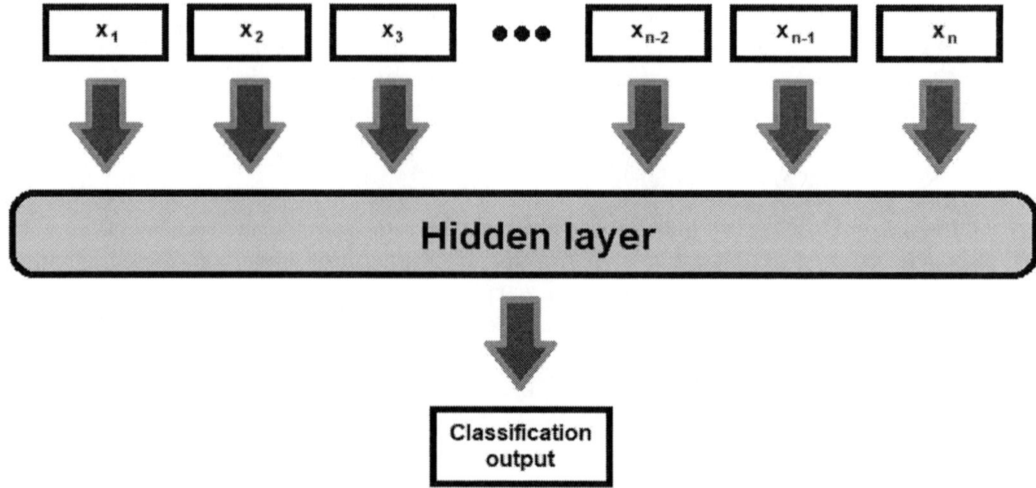

Figure 3: FastText architecture used for our multi-label text classification with n-gram features $x_1, x_2, x_3, ..., x_{n-2}, x_{n-1}, x_n$.

3.4 Whole Leaflets Categorization Pipeline

The diagram presented in Fig. 4 illustrates the overall setup of the solution for the whole leaflets categorization pipeline. An image corresponding to a digital leaflet is received as the input of the system. In the first step, the descriptions related to products are initially identified over the leaflet image using the previously trained region detection model. The detected regions are used for generating the masked image that is used in the text recognition stage to extract the texts of interest for each promotion. Finally, the model for text classification is applied for each description in order to compute the final output, which contains the categories associated for each promotion.

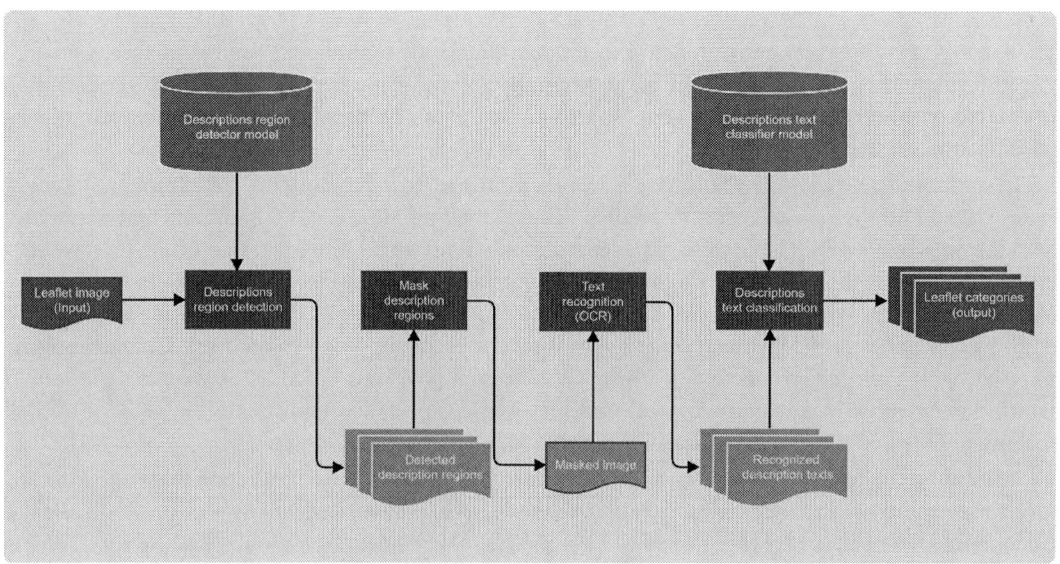

Figure 4: Diagram of the whole leaflets categorization pipeline.

4 Experiments and Results

With the aim of validating the proposed approach in a specific leaflets categorization use case, we prepared a set of experiments with leaflets data captured by Nielsen. In this section, we describe the experimental setup: the datasets, the hyperparameters used for training and the comparative results with different data and approaches.

4.1 Leaflets Dataset

To the best of our knowledge, there are not public datasets with GT information for leaflets categorization over images of catalogs, so we used our own labeled datasets from Nielsen internal data. We applied two different leaflets datasets for training and evaluation. Firstly, a "base" dataset with leaflets from only one retailer with textual descriptions in English. Secondly, a extended dataset with leaflets from four retailers with varied image formats to test generalization, and texts from two languages (English and French) to evaluate the multi-lingual capabilities of our approach. As the datasets are composed of proprietary images, we can not publicly share them. However, the main properties and statistics from both datasets are summarized in Table 1. It must be noted that the data distribution is long-tailed and thus unbalanced for both training and validation/test splits, as shown in Fig. 5. Then, this is an extra challenge for our models in order to be robust against the typical problems derived from long-tail datasets.

Dataset	#Languages	#Retailers	#Images	#Samples	#Categories	Avg. samples per cat.	Std. samples per cat.
Base	1	1	449	10,333	382	27.05	100.75
Extended	2	4	1,079	20,646	504	40.96	189.79

Table 1: Main statistics about the leaflets categorization datasets used for training and evaluation.

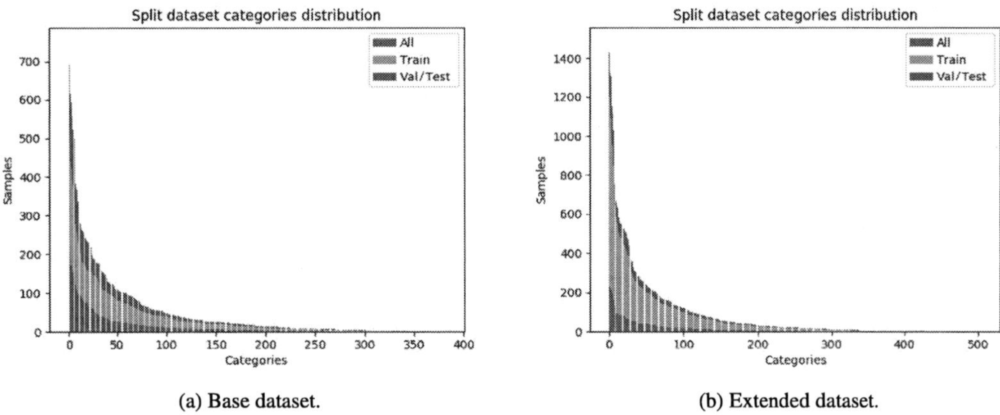

(a) Base dataset.

(b) Extended dataset.

Figure 5: Distribution of category samples for the used leaflets datasets.

4.2 Hyperparameters Tuning

Region detection and text classification models require some hyperparameters tuning to obtain the best possible results. Some standard hyperparameters typically used in these models are configured.

In region detection, we decided to train our models using pre-trained weights on ImageNet (Deng et al., 2009) and based on a ResNet-101 backbone (He et al., 2016). Anchor scales and ratios for RPN are important hyperparameters, which are configured as $[2, 4, 8]$ and $[0.5, 1, 2]$, respectively. Learning rate was set to $1 \cdot 10^{-6}$ and regularization is applied by means of dropout (keep probabilities mode), which is set to 0.7. Besides, an Adam optimizer (Kingma and Ba, 2015) is used. A confidence threshold of 0.4 is applied to discard bounding boxes with low confidences. Trainings are iterated during 100 epochs.

The multi-label text classification hyperparameters configuration has a great dependence on the number of n-grams, which is a value finally set to 3 based on previous cross-validation experiments. Besides, the learning rate is set to 0.1 with a learning update rate of 100. A confidence threshold of 0.25 is applied to identify the categories of interest for a specific product description. We train for 30 epochs.

4.3 Results in Leaflets Categorization

In order to evaluate the performance of our approach, we apply metrics based on precision, recall and accuracy. Besides, we also use these metrics to obtain comparative results with respect to a standard baseline text classification, which is based on directly extracting OCR paragraphs on the wild from the image, without previously using a RPN detector for filtering texts related to product descriptions. In this baseline case, the texts recognized by the OCR with all the class probabilities below the text classifier confidence threshold are not considered as descriptions. Overall test results comparison is presented in Table 2 for the base dataset. As can be seen in these results, our approach yields an accuracy improvement of 24 points with respect to the standard baseline. These results confirm the enhancement given by our system with respect to the proposed baseline.

Method	Precision	Recall	Accuracy
Baseline (OCR on the wild + text classification)	0.64	0.66	0.48
Ours (RPN + OCR masked + text classification)	**0.86**	**0.81**	**0.72**

Table 2: Overall test results comparing a standard baseline approach vs ours in the base leaflets dataset.

It must be remarked that a confidence threshold of 0.25 is used for the multi-label text classification model of our proposal. This confidence represents the probabilities of having a correct prediction for a class, so the confidence threshold is used to filter predictions with low probabilities. The specific confidence threshold value is obtained by maximizing the accuracy values over threshold iterations from 0.00 to 1.00, as can be seen in the graph presented in Fig. 6 (b). To make fair comparisons, we also set the confidence threshold for the maximized accuracy value of the standard baseline approach, which is 0.40. The threshold iteration graph for the baseline method is shown in Fig. 6 (a).

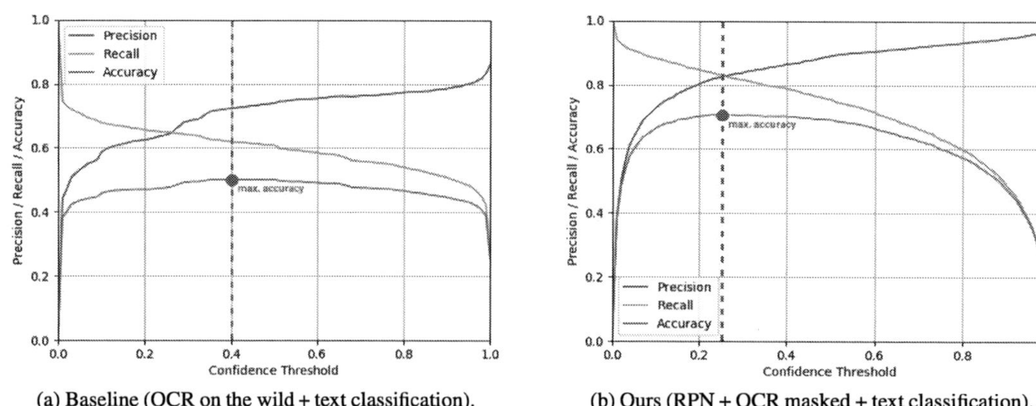

(a) Baseline (OCR on the wild + text classification).　　　(b) Ours (RPN + OCR masked + text classification).

Figure 6: Graphs about sliding confidence threshold in text classification for the base leaflets dataset.

As a final insight about results, we trained our models using the extended dataset to check out how it generalizes to more retailers and languages. The obtained results can be seen in Table 3, where the models trained in the extended dataset are having a better performance in test. Moreover, in Fig. 7 we depict some qualitative results about some leaflets and their corresponding predictions. According to these results, it seems that the embeddings for the text classifier are able to generalize categorization to new languages. The reported accuracies must be understood taking into account the long-tail problems of the dataset exposed in Fig. 5, so the classes with less training samples are more difficult to predict.

Dataset	Precision	Recall	Accuracy
Base	0.86	0.81	0.72
Extended	**0.87**	**0.86**	**0.76**

Table 3: Comparison of results for our method in the base and extended leaflets datasets.

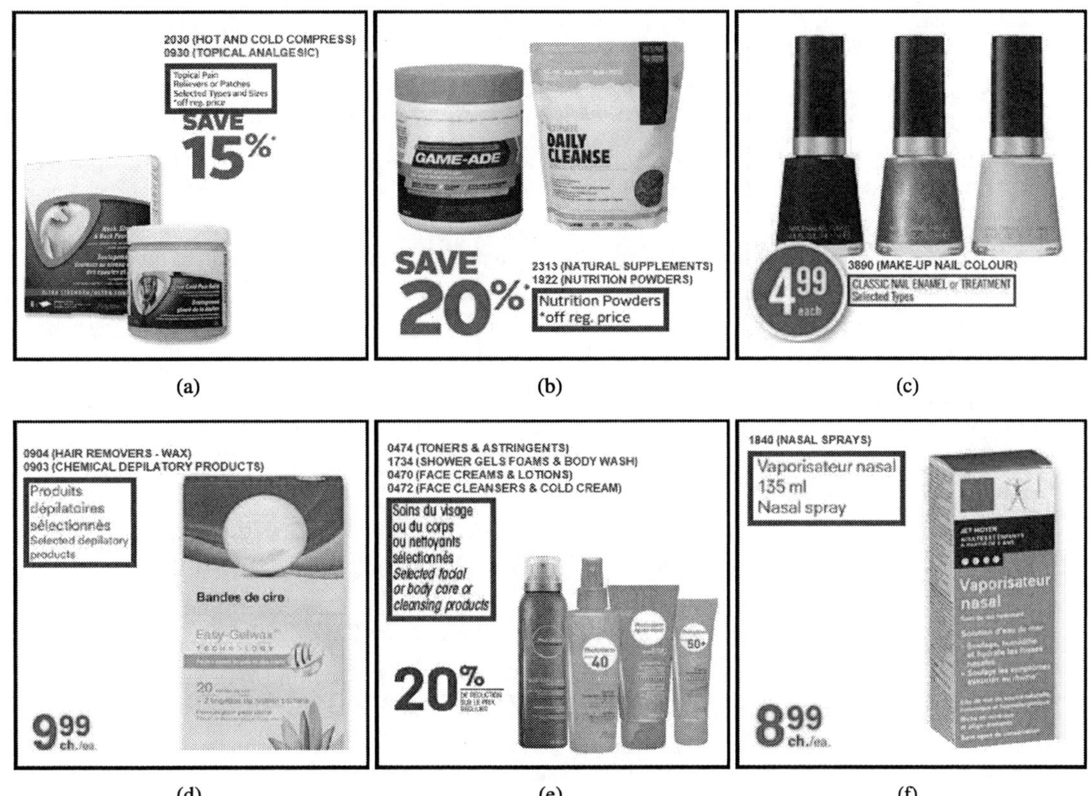

(a)   (b)   (c)

(d)   (e)   (f)

Figure 7: Qualitative results about leaflets examples and their corresponding predictions.

5 Conclusions

Along this paper, we have presented for the first time in the e-commerce research community (to the best of our knowledge) the problem of automated product coding for digital leaflets. In particular, we have addressed the problem of product classification for each promotion using image detection and multi-label text classification techniques. This schema provides a final proposal in the intersection between CV and NLP domains. Experimental results show that the described approach consistently outperforms a standard baseline in all the evaluated scenarios.

Future research includes expanding the multi-label classification of each promotion to knowledge extraction of different attributes, such as brand and product names, quantities, volumes, price or discounts. The final goal of this research line is to extract all the possible information contained in digital leaflets in order to fully understand their whole context.

We believe that the automated product coding in digital leaflets is at an early research stage but yet it is a very interesting approach in the future of e-commerce. Then, this paper has contributed the initial milestones for the dissemination and enhancement of this research topic across the e-commerce research community.

References

S. Antol, A. Agrawal, J. Lu, M. Mitchell, D. Batra, C. L. Zitnick, and D. Parikh. 2015. VQA: Visual Question Answering. In *International Conference on Computer Vision (ICCV)*, pages 2425–2433.

R. Arroyo, J. Tovar, F. J. Delgado, E. J. Almazan, D. G. Serrador, and A. Hurtado. 2019. Integration of Text-Maps in CNNs for Region Detection among Different Textual Categories. In *Workshops of Conference on Computer Vision and Pattern Recognition (CVPR)*, pages 1–4.

X. Bai, M. Yang, P. Lyu, Y. Xu, and Jiebo Luo. 2018. Integrating Scene Text and Visual Appearance for Fine-Grained Image Classification. *IEEE Access*, 6:66322–66335.

J. Deng, W. Dong, R. Socher, L. Li, K. Li, and F. Li. 2009. ImageNet: A large-scale hierarchical image database. In *Conference on Computer Vision and Pattern Recognition (CVPR)*, pages 248–255.

J. Devlin, M. Chang, K. Lee, and K. Toutanova. 2018. BERT: Pre-training of Deep Bidirectional Transformers for Language Understanding. In *Conference of the North American Chapter of the Association for Computational Linguistics (NAACL-HLT)*, pages 4171–4186.

L. Gomez, A. Mafla, M. Rusinol, and D. Karatzas. 2018. Single Shot Scene Text Retrieval. In *European Conference on Computer Vision (ECCV)*, pages 728–744.

K. He, X. Zhang, S. Ren, and J. Sun. 2016. Deep Residual Learning for Image Recognition. In *Conference on Computer Vision and Pattern Recognition (CVPR)*, pages 770–778.

A. Joulin, E. Grave, P. Bojanowski, and T. Mikolov. 2017. Bag of Tricks for Efficient Text Classification. In *Conference of the European Chapter of the Association for Computational Linguistics (EACL)*, pages 427–431.

D. P. Kingma and J. Ba. 2015. Adam: A Method for Stochastic Optimization. In *International Conference on Learning Representations (ICLR)*, pages 1–15.

A. Krizhevsky, I. Sutskever, and G. E. Hinton. 2012. ImageNet Classification with Deep Convolutional Neural Networks. In *International Conference on Neural Information Processing Systems (NIPS)*, pages 1106–1114.

C. Lee and S. Osindero. 2016. Recursive Recurrent Nets with Attention Modeling for OCR in the Wild. In *Conference on Computer Vision and Pattern Recognition (CVPR)*, pages 2231–2239.

W. Liu, D. Anguelov, D. Erhan, C. Szegedy, S. E. Reed, C. Fu, and A. C. Berg. 2016. SSD: Single Shot MultiBox Detector. In *European Conference on Computer Vision (ECCV)*, pages 21–37.

J. Lu, D. Batra, D. Parikh, and S. Lee. 2019. ViLBERT: Pretraining Task-Agnostic Visiolinguistic Representations for Vision-and-Language Tasks. In *International Conference on Neural Information Processing Systems (NIPS)*, pages 13–23.

J. Redmon, S. Divvala, R. Girshick, and A. Farhadi. 2016. You Only Look Once: Unified, Real-Time Object Detection. In *Conference on Computer Vision and Pattern Recognition (CVPR)*, pages 779–788.

S. Ren, K. He, R. Girshick, and J. Sun. 2015. Faster R-CNN: Towards Real-Time Object Detection with Region Proposal Networks. In *International Conference on Neural Information Processing Systems (NIPS)*, pages 91–99.

H. Rezatofighi, N. Tsoi, J. Gwak, A. Sadeghian, I. Reid, and S. Savarese. 2019. Generalized Intersection over Union: A Metric and A Loss for Bounding Box Regression. In *Conference on Computer Vision and Pattern Recognition (CVPR)*, pages 658–666.

R. Rothe, M. Guillaumin, and L. van Gool. 2014. Non-maximum Suppression for Object Detection by Passing Messages Between Windows. In *Asian Conference on Computer Vision (ACCV)*, pages 290–306.

W. Su, X. Zhu, Y. Cao, Li B, L. Lu, F. Wei, and J. Dai. 2020. VL-BERT: Pre-training of Generic Visual Linguistic Representations. In *International Conference on Learning Representations (ICLR)*, pages 1–16.

A. Vaswani, N. Shazeer, N. Parmar, J. Uszkoreit, L. Jones, A. N. Gomez, L. Kaiser, and I. Polosukhin. 2017. Attention is All you Need. In *International Conference on Neural Information Processing Systems (NIPS)*, pages 5998–6008.

C. Wick, C. Reul, and F. Puppe. 2020. Calamari - A High-Performance Tensorflow-based Deep Learning Package for Optical Character Recognition. *Digital Humanities Quarterly*.

E. Zacharias, M. Teuchler, and B. Bernier. 2020. Image Processing Based Scene-Text Detection and Recognition with Tesseract. *arXiv (CoRR)*.

Bilingual Transfer Learning for Online Product Classification

Erik Lehmann, András Simonyi
Frankfurt School of Finance
erik.lehmann91@gmail.com
andras.simonyi@gmail.com

Lukas Henkel, Jörn Franke
European Central Bank
lukas.henkel@ecb.europa.eu
jorn.franke@ecb.europa.eu

Abstract

Consumer Price Indices (CPIs) are one of the major statistics produced by Statistical Offices, and of crucial importance to Central Banks. Nowadays prices of many consumer goods can be obtained online, enabling a much more detailed measurement of inflation rates. One major challenge is to classify the variety of products from different shops and languages into the given statistical schema consisting of a complex multi-level classification hierarchy - the European Classification of Individual Consumption according to Purpose (ECOICOP) for European countries, since there is no model, mapping or labeled data available. We focus in our analysis on food, beverage and tobacco which account for 74 of the 258 ECOICOP categories and 19 % of the Euro Area inflation basket. In this paper we build a classifier on web scraped, hand-labeled product data from German retailers and transfer to French data using cross lingual word embeddings. We compare its performance against a classifier trained on single languages and a classifier with both languages trained jointly. Furthermore, we propose a pipeline to effectively create a data set with balanced labels using transferred predictions and active learning. In addition, we test how much data it takes to build a single language classifier from scratch and if there are benefits from multilingual training. Our proposed system reduces the time to complete the task by about two thirds.

1 Introduction

Consumer price inflation in the euro area is measured by the Harmonised Index of Consumer Prices (HICP), which is calculated based on a basket of goods and services. While prices for some goods, like energy prices, are easy to observe, prices for many product groups, like e.g. food, are often collected manually. This survey-based approach is relatively expensive and slow. Nowadays we have access to data on prices of individual products sold on the internet. This kind of data can help to improve the quality of the data and monitor it at a higher frequency. There are various initiatives working on the usage of alternative data sources for the calculation of price statistics, but these are mainly country-specific. Examples are the use of scanner data (Białek and Berkesewicz, 2020) and web scraped food data (Macias and Stelmasiak, 2019) to measure Polish inflation, the measurement of the CPI in Finland (Koskimäki and Ylä-Jarkko, 2003) or forecasting daily CPI in the United Kingdom (Powell et al., 2018). The billion prices project (Cavallo and Rigobon, 2016) extensively researched this topic and validated the usefulness by backtesting against traditional measured price indices. Furthermore, they use online prices also to answer macroeconomic research questions, like the verification of inflation statistics from Argentina or the review of effects from changes in US trade policy (Cavallo et al., 2019).

There is an important problem related to online price data, which is rarely addressed but always encountered in the process: the classification of millions of online products into categories. This is crucial for analysing the individual components underlying inflation as required by consumer price indexes. Those classification systems are rather complex with hundreds of categories within several layers of hierarchy. Usually experts in the specific classification system are needed and the classification cannot

Disclaimer: This paper solely expresses the opinion of the authors. Their views do not necessarily reflect those of the ECB.

21

Proceedings of the Workshop on Natural Language Processing in E-Commerce (EComNLP), pages 21–31
Barcelona, Spain (Online), Dec 12, 2020.

be done by people without this expertise. Additionally, the product set is not static. During our investigation of scraped web product data, we found out that products are phased out and new products appear frequently. Thus over time much more different products with the same or completely different characteristics appear than originally available and a lot of them disappear again, meaning that constant monitoring of the system is necessary.

Using supervised machine learning methods to automatize a classification task of this type often requires a large amount of labeled training data and labeling by hand is very time consuming as it needs to be done for every language individually. Moreover, all the texts (product names, descriptions and categories) have to be represented by numerical features or feature vectors, which leads into the field of natural language processing (NLP). Many of the previously mentioned initiatives have neglected a detailed classification or only offer very broad classifications. This makes them less suitable for analysing individual inflation components. Furthermore, they do not take into account the fact that product data can be available in different languages, which is especially important for the polyglot European market.

In this study we address how contemporary NLP and machine learning techniques can be used to automate the classification of online products, and what kind of effort is needed to build a model from scratch without having labeled training data. The underlying classification system is the European Classification of Individual Consumption according to Purpose (ECOICOP) (European Union, 2016) used by the European Statistic offices and the European Union.

We found the vocabulary of the product texts to be very domain specific and pretrained language models only to cover parts. For this reason we have been working on ways to extend the vocabulary of existing models, which limited the methods we could use.

In particular, we look at ways of transferring knowledge contained in a classification model for product data in one language to another using cross-lingual word embeddings. In addition, we propose different neural architectures for monolingual training, bilingual transfer and bilingual training. We also report how much labeled data is needed for a decent model and compare the results of zero-shot bilingual transfer to bilingual training. On the basis of our findings we propose an active learning pipeline to create balanced training data in a target language. The goal is to build a tool-set for a multi-lingual collection of web-scraped product corpora to make product classification accessible in many languages.

2 Data

2.1 ECOICOP Classification System

Consumer inflation and CPI in the euro area are based on the ECOICOP schema. The classification schema has different hierarchies; we focus on the five-digit level, which consist of 258 different categories and is identical for all countries in the euro area. The 5-digit level distinguishes between, e.g., "rice", "bread" or "pasta products and couscous" which all belong to the category "bread and cereals" at the four-digit level. The 5-digit level is currently used for the calculation of the CPI and inflation (Eurostat, 2020).

We limit our analysis to the following two two-digit categories and hierarchical subcategories up to the 5-digit level, because those match our scraped data from supermarket websites:

- food and non-alcoholic beverages (01.)

- alcoholic beverages and tobacco (02.)

Together they account for 74 of the 258 ECOICOP 5-digit categories and 19% of the euro area inflation basket. All other items are classified as non-food.

The task of COICOP classification of products cannot be delegated to anyone. The classification system is complex and requires expertise in food classification as the categories are described using a language/concepts that only statistic experts understand. Furthermore, expert classification ensures also more consistency in the classification of products. An example of an ECOICOP 5 digit category is the following:

- Food and non-alcoholic beverages (01.)

ECOICOP category	# of observations
9999 Non-Food	9,396
1171 Fresh or chilled vegetables [...]	1,182
2121 Wine from grapes	1,177
⋮	⋮
2123 Fortified wines	23
2202 Cigars	10
2112 Alcoholic soft drinks	8

Table 1: COICOP categories observations

- Food (01.1)
    * Bread and Cereals (01.1.1)
        · Pizza and quiche (01.1.1.5)

2.2 Product Data

The product data is scraped from selected online shops of supermarkets in Germany, France and Belgium. The products sold by different supermarkets are similar, but each website provides different information or categorization. In particular, we use the product name and category given by the supermarket. For example, a product name from a German supermarket would be "Eiweiß Toastbrötchen" and a supermarket category would be "Lebensmittel / Frühstück / Brot / Brötchen". Both contain very specialised terminology that are usually not found in many public corpora, especially brand names or special food descriptions. For example, the German word "Zitronenglasur" (lemon glaze) does not exist currently in the German Wikipedia, but is commonly found in supermarkets. Furthermore, the supermarket category can usually not be mapped to COICOP. In addition, we extracted words from the product URLs as they often provide additional information.

For many products we have further information like product description, producer, brand, quantity or ingredients. However, due to their variability, especially across shops, we did not include them in our current research.

We do some basic preprocessing steps on the text including tokenizing, lowercasing and replacing special characters and numbers with the goal of reducing the vocabulary and making it more language independent. The texts from name, categorization and URL are concatenated with a separator token <sep> in between. The average German text consists of 19 tokens, while the average French text of 28 tokens. We classified 31,000 random products of eight German supermarkets and 22,000 products from two French supermarkets, two thirds by hand and one third rule based with manual validation. The appearance of products per category is imbalanced, with a mean of 419 products per class for the German data (see Table 1).

The French data is distributed similarly, as a difference we do not have tobacco products. The reason for this category imbalance is the products' imbalanced occurrence on the shop websites, i.e. the distribution corresponds to what is available in reality.

3 Related Work

Although there is interest for detailed inflation monitoring, only a small amount of research exists about classification into the ECOICOP or similar schemes for online product data. For example, the billion prices project emphasize the use of big data for inflation measurement (Cavallo and Rigobon (2016)). They collected web scraped data from large multi-channel retailers in the United States and built a Naive Bayes classifier on "language-specific, hand-categorized items". To our knowledge there is just a single study on using vector representations of words in the context of COICOP classification: Martindale et al. (2019) take web scraped clothing data and use a semi-supervised approach to create training labels for their products. They useed various methods to spread existing labels. They found them to be correctly classified in 70% of all cases.

Text classification.   Text classification is one of the core NLP tasks with a huge number of applications (e.g., sentiment analysis, spam filtering, and intent detection in chatbots to mention some of the most important ones). Specifically, the classification of short texts that do not necessarily consist of a well-formed sentence or sentences is also a much-studied problem (Wang et al., 2017; Saha et al., 2019; Chen et al., 2019). State-of-the-art short text classification models typically consist of a deep neural architecture on top of a static word or subword embedding layer. While recurrent neural nets (RNNs) using long short-term memory (LSTM) (Hochreiter and Schmidhuber, 1997) are often the first choice for sequential data like time series or texts, one-dimensional convolutional neural networks (CNNs) were found to outperform LSTM-based RNN variants in many settings, especially in the case of short or unstructured texts (Lee and Dernoncourt, 2016; Seo et al., 2020).

Transfer learning.   Using representations learned for a supervised task on a large data set as a basis for building and training a model for a different data set is a frequently used method for addressing data scarcity problems. One of the first models widely used for this kind of transfer learning was the AlexNet convolutional image classifier by Krizhevsky et al. (2012). For the transfer the upper layers are cut off while lower layers get frozen and on top of them new layers are trained on the new task. Word embeddings are another example where representations trained on one task (to predict a word given its surrounding) are used for many other tasks. Originally, an important limitation of pre-trained word embeddings was their limited vocabulary, since they provided representations only for words that occurred in the training corpus. To overcome this limitation, Facebook AI Research additionally trained their embedding model on certain subwords occurring in the corpus as well (Bojanowski et al., 2017). The resulting framework (fastText) provides models pre-trained on Wikipedia for a large amount of languages. Klementiev et al. (2012) trained word embeddings jointly for English and German to obtain representations in one common vector space. Transferring knowledge from a classifier only trained on English data to a classifier for German data using these cross-lingual word vectors outperformed a simple translation approach. In the following section we use a common vector space for French and German to transfer the ECOICOP classification. A very successful approach for cross-lingual zero shot learning was introduced by Eriguchi et al. (2018). They used state-of-the-art transformer-based language models trained on multiple languages. Only the encoder part of the model was transferred, why the decoder was replaced with their own classification layer with impressive results in transferring the learned information between English and French. Earlier, Johnson et al. (2017) already showed that a single Neural Machine Translation model trained on multiple languages can generalize to some extent, allowing for zero shot prediction on unseen data.

4   Framework

We propose a CNN architecture (cf. Figure 2) on top of word vector representations exemplified in Figure 1.

4.1   Results

We start with a discussion of cross-lingual word embeddings and methods of extending the vocabulary to take into account the specialised vocabulary found in our product data. Then we describe the network architecture based on a convolutional neural network and the aforementioned embeddings. Finally, we present results obtained by using single language training, by using transfer learning from German to French, and by multilingual joint training of the model on both languages. The NLP research of the last few years has been dominated by the rise of the transformer neural architecture, also for multilingual problems (Johnson et al., 2017). For our specific problem the typically used pretrained transformer models were not suitable because there is no straightforward way to include domain specific vocabulary.

4.2   Cross-lingual Embeddings

Context.   Word embeddings represent words in a high-dimensional vector space in which semantic relations between words correspond to geometric relationships. The embeddings are trained on the task

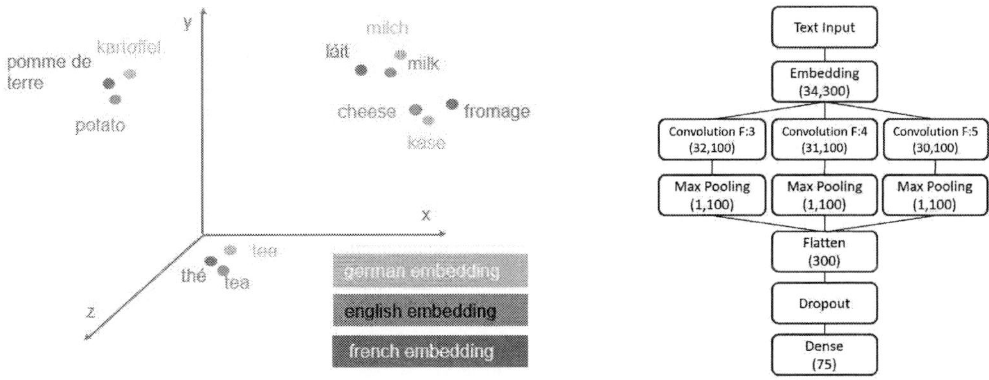

Figure 1: Artificial joint plot of different embedding models

Figure 2: CNN architecture following the example of Kim (2014)

of predicting a word given its context, thereby, indirectly, a joint probability distribution of words is also learned. The learned vector representations capture both syntactic and semantic properties of words because they have to represent all information about words that is useful for the prediction task. As these syntactic and semantic properties are often similar across languages, word vectors from different languages can be aligned into one common space in which cross-lingual semantic and syntactic relations are also represented by geometric ones. The alignment is typically realized by applying a linear mapping between the two vector spaces (Mikolov et al., 2013). This mapping is often learned in a supervised manner by using a bilingual dictionary or parallel texts with the objective of minimizing the distances between the representations of corresponding word pairs (Zou et al., 2013). In general, it is not possible to align word vectors perfectly between languages because all of the texts the model is trained on and all of the semantic relations have a cultural background. It is even possible to observe cultural processes in texts from different points in times (Kozlowski et al., 2019). This also applies to our problem, e.g., while it is common in Germany to have savoury dishes for breakfast, in France sweet breakfasts are strongly preferred. The fact that word embeddings represent cultural characteristics has the consequence that they can also amplify biases, e.g. gender stereotypes (Bolukbasi et al., 2016). Fortunately, for our analysis this is of minor importance as we deal with food product data, which does not seem to be affected by such biases.

Fine-tuning pretrained embeddings. We use aligned Multilingual Unsupervised and Supervised Embeddings (MUSE) by Joulin et al. (2018), who make use of a Generative Adversarial Network and Procrustes for fine-tuning. They outperform other embedding models on many benchmark tasks (Joulin et al., 2018). When using the embeddings for training we make use of the existence of shared word forms in the vocabularies like *pizza*. In fact, 13% of the German word forms covered by the MUSE embeddings also appears in the French MUSE embeddings' vocabulary. For these shared words we calculate the average embedding vector and afterwards we combine both embedding spaces into one with the effect that the shared vocabulary will already be fine-tuned to the task, and this fine-tuning is directly transferred as the French model uses the same embedding space.
The pre-trained German embeddings cover only 47% and the French 75% of unique tokens in data. Subword embeddings are not provided with the published MUSE models, and, at least for transfer learning, aligning sub-words is a topic of its own since they carry much more syntactic then semantic information (Kayi et al., 2020).

Expanding Vocabularies using K-Nearest-Neighbour (KNN). We generate embeddings for words not covered by the pre-trained MUSE embedding vocabularies based on their distribution in our data set using a KNN approach (cf. Algorithm 1). Specifically, we trained a fastText model using the Gensim implementation (Řehůřek and Sojka, 2010) on 500,000 German and 330,000 French web scraped products.

While this amount of data is not sufficient to learn good semantics, the model still learns statistics which is especially important for the morphologically rich German language. It is an open research problem on how many web scraped products we would need to benefit significantly more, but our results, as we will see later, are still very good with the given data set.

From our own and the pre-trained fastText models we build a list of words that appeared in both models. This shared vocabulary is, in turn, used to generate MUSE-aligned embeddings for words in the data set that are not in the MUSE vocabulary. The aligned word vectors are calculated as a distance-weighted average of the MUSE embeddings of the shared vocabulary words that are nearest in the embedding space of our trained fastText model.

Algorithm 1 KNN-WEIGHTED-AVG-VECTORS(P, L, K)

Require: P, a dictionary with pre-trained word embeddings (keys are words, values the corresponding vectors); L, a dictionary with embeddings trained locally on the data set; K, number of nearest neighbours to consider

 1: $SharedVocab \leftarrow P.keys \cap L.keys$
 2: $OutOfVocab \leftarrow L.keys \setminus SharedVocab$
 3: **for all** o in $OutOfVocab$ **do**
 4:     $SD \leftarrow [\ ]$
 5:     **for all** s in $SharedVocab$ **do**
 6:         $SD \leftarrow SD \oplus \langle \textsc{Distance}(L[o], L[s]), s \rangle$
 7:     **end for**
 8:     $SD \leftarrow \textsc{Sort}(SD)$ $\triangleright$ sort increasing by distance
 9:     $\mathbf{v} \leftarrow \mathbf{0}$
10:     **for** $i = 1$ to K **do**
11:         $d, s \leftarrow SD_i$
12:         $\mathbf{p} \leftarrow P[s]$
13:         $\mathbf{v} \leftarrow \mathbf{v} + d\mathbf{p}$
14:     **end for**
15:     $\mathbf{v} \leftarrow \textsc{Normalize}(\mathbf{v})$ $\triangleright$ e.g., to have 1.0 L2 norm
16:     $P[o] \leftarrow \mathbf{v}$ $\triangleright$ extend the pre-trained embeddings
17: **end for**

4.3 Network Architecture

We use MUSE embeddings extended by the method outlined in the previous subsection to represent the product texts. The classifier model itself is based on the aforementioned fastText framework. Since prediction of ECOICOP categories on the 5-digit level has never been done before for web scraped supermarket products, we investigate how well the classes can be predicted and how much labeled data is necessary in order to achieve satisfactory results. We differentiate between single language models, single language models for transfer learning and multilingual models. For the classification of the web scraped text strings we trained and tested different neural net architectures using the enriched MUSE embeddings as base.

Preparation. For the single language case we fine-tune word vectors during model training to adjust to the problem. The input sequences have a length of 34 tokens, which is the 95% quantile for our texts. Shorter documents are padded with zero vectors. To address the class imbalance we apply class weights to our network which are calculated as

$$weight_{class} = N/(C \cdot N_{class}),$$

where N is the number of products, C the number of classes and N_{class} the number of products in the class in question. The calculated class weights are taken into account during the learning phase. We train our model stepwise on 250, 500, 2,000, 10,000, 15,000 (French), and 25,000 (German) data points to report the fit at different levels. When training multilingual models we take the whole data of the source language while adding stepwise data of the target language. We oversample the target language in addition to balance the data. We split our data into training, validation, and test data sets. The held out test set includes products which appear neither in the training nor in the validation set. Therefore, we also measure the effect of changing product ranges.

Language	Train	Validation	Test
German	23,597	3,933	3,933
French	17,124	2,854	2,854

Table 2: Number of data points available for training, validation and test

Convolutional Neural Network. We make use of the idea to treat our products, represented as a sequence of vectors, as an image with the size $sequence\_length \times embedding\_dimension$ and use convolutions to extract features. This method was first used by Kim (2014). Using this technique the training can be fully parallelized and has today replaced RNNs in many NLP tasks (Gehring et al., 2017). We use multiple convolutional filters which move through the input sequence with the kernel looking at n tokens ($n \in \{3, 4, 5\}$) and all embedding coordinates (with a kernel size of $n \times 300$) at a time as proposed by Kim (2014). The used CNN looks at context windows of up to five words (Wang et al., 2018) and recognizes short-range dependencies, does not learn long-range dependencies as RNNs can. This reflects the characteristics of our data well. The outputs of the convolutions are pooled using maximum pooling, and the resulting outputs are concatenated and flattened into a one-dimensional vector. To regularize the network we apply dropout to 50% of the connections before the final dense layer which outputs a probability distribution over the 75 categories using softmax activation (Wang et al., 2018).

Single language training. Results of single language training with max pooling and trainable (non-static) embeddings, and average pooling with static embeddings for German on the test data are presented in Table 3.

Similarly, results for single language training on the French test data are presented in Table 4.

N	250	500	2,000	10,000	25,000
CNN_{max}	59.9	78.29	92.0	96.0	97.4
CNN_{avg}	58.8	63.2	88.3	94.2	95.3

N	250	500	2,000	10,000	15,000
CNN_{max}	58.5	82.8	90.8	95.0	96.2
CNN_{avg}	54.4	71.5	89.5	94.0	94.6

Table 3: Accuracy on test data - training the CNN model on N German products in percent

Table 4: Accuracy on test data training the CNN model on N French products in percent

For the German data we classified 96.0% of the test products correctly, training on 10,000 data points with max pooling. Our best French model reached 95.0% accuracy, trained on 10,000 data points with max pooling. Overall, the training curve is steep and the model learns even on small data. In addition, the training process is rather stable.

Transfer learning. Having built the classifier on our German product data set we want to make use of the MUSE property that the embeddings for individual languages are cross-lingually aligned, and reuse the German model on our French data. In particular, we examine the prospects of directly transferring knowledge by predicting the category of French products without the model having seen French data before (zero shot learning) and we also experiment with fine-tuning the German model with a small amount of French product data (few shot learning). To make this work we have to make a few changes to our model. Most important is the freezing of our word vectors. While we had them fine-tuned during single language training, now we need to ensure that they stay aligned. To further train the the model on French data we cut the last layer of the German model and replace it with a new initialized layer. In Table 5 we report scores both using max and average pooling layers.

Comparing the results with single language training we observe that, especially for cases where there is little training data available (up to 1,000 examples), transfer learning brings significant advantage compared to training models only on the corresponding monolingual data for each language.

Multilingual training. Results also confirm a higher advantage when both languages are trained jointly (cf. Table 6). Initially, with few samples, this is much higher then later when more training data is available. However, even then a small advantage can be observed.

N	0	100	250	1,000	5,000
CNN_{max}	42.0	63.9	78.7	87.4	93.3
CNN_{avg}	38.0	60.0	77.8	88.7	93.7

Table 5: Accuracy on test data training the transferred CNN model on N French products in percent

N	250	500	2,000	10,000	25,000
German	65.8	78.6	90.7	95.9	97.8
French	74.6	82.2	91.6	96.0	98.2

Table 6: Accuracy on test data training the CNN model on N French and German products in percent

Summary. We present in Figure 3 a comparison of all training approaches we experimented with. The CNN SL learning curve corresponds to the approach of using single-language training. CNN ML describes multi-language training, and the remaining curves show the characteristics of transfer learning, with static (CNN SE) and non-static embeddings (CNN NSE). Transfer learning has been shown to only

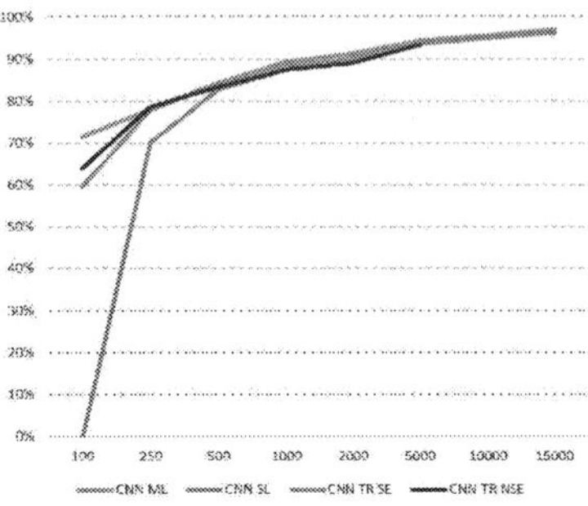

Figure 3: Accuracy on test data training the CNN models on N French products, single language training (CNN SL), multi language training (CNN ML), transfer learning with static embedding (CNN SE) and non-static (CNN NSE), in percent

Figure 4: Labeling tool with a drop-down list to select the category one wants to label, information about the product and drop-down to select the correct label, pre-filled with the model's prediction

partially transfer results from German to French. Transferred models cannot be used for automation without additional supervised training, but can still provide predictions useful in certain settings, e.g. as annotation aids, as will be shown in the next section. In contrast, the joint German and French training achieved very good results and outperformed French single language training on every amount of data as well as the results from transfer learning. Especially when trained on all data available the multi language training raised the result by 2%. We therefore see an improvement for the low resource language when trained jointly.

5 Active Learning

Motivation. The main idea of active learning is to achieve higher model performance on the same amount of data or the same performance on less data by letting the learning algorithm choose which data points to label and train on. Using this approach we can take advantage of our transferred results to reduce annotation costs when transferring to other European and non-European languages.

Active learning is an active research field and strategies often differ for certain use cases. Methods suitable for our problem belong to the field of pool-based sampling (Settles, 2009) as we have a large pool of web-scraped products and it has to be decided which products should be labeled. One popular sampling strategy is uncertainty sampling: this approach always labels and learns from the data point the model is most uncertain about, with the goal to concentrate on the observation from which the model can acquire the maximal amount of new information:

$$x_{least\ confident} =_x P(\hat{y}|x).$$

This strategy is often refined by taking the distance to the second most likely class as measurement. This variant is called margin sampling (Settles, 2009). The exact opposite is suitable for our zero shot prediction. As we start without annotated data, every observation in the new language is valuable in the beginning and we use the ones we are most certain about. To sample from different ECOICOP classes we condition the sampling on highest prediction certainty for a specific class.

Enhancing the annotation process for new languages. In this context, our transfer learning results give valuable input. The data creation process means adapting the classifier to a new language without having any labeled data. While uncertainty sampling is often used to find training examples where the model learns most, at the beginning of the annotation process every observation is valuable. Hence, we propose the following approach:

1. At the beginning we use zero shot predictions from the existing (transferred) model to create label proposals and use certainty sampling, i.e. select the ones the model is most certain about and present it to the human annotator for confirmation. This saves significantly time for annotating the first examples.

2. As we have shown above, the learning curve is very steep. Already 250 annotated observations increased the accuracy to 80%, which is double the rate of zero shot learning. After retraining the model with the 250 annotated examples, we switch to conditional certainty sampling and label further data points chosen both on the basis of the model's certainty and with the aim of generating an equally distributed data set which is beneficial for training.

3. In the last step, we propose to select the data points from which the classifier can learn the most, i.e. where it is most uncertain, using uncertainty sampling.

Labeling tool. We present in Figure 4 a screenshot of our labeling tool that implements the aforementioned process. Based on a given data set of unlabeled products, it tries to predict the correct labeling according to ECOICOP (5 digits) and presents this to the user. The user can simply look if it makes sense for the description, and when in doubt they can also open the product URL. If the label is correct then the human annotator simply clicks save and can continue with the next product. Otherwise the annotator needs to select the correct category. Since ECOICOP is hierarchical the annotator might simply select the correct label from another nearby category at a higher level, i.e., a label close to the predicted one.

Preliminary results. The benefits of the labeling tool were measured in a preliminary evaluation setup by two human annotators for French product data. Their feedback indicated that by using the proposals based on zero-shot learning they could accelerate the annotation process by a magnitude of 2. After retraining the classifier with the newly annotated data (ca. 1,000 labels) they could increase annotation speed by a magnitude of 3. This means just 20-30% of the time is needed compared to random annotation. These results are very encouraging, although a more thorough investigation is required with more languages as well as non-food ECOICOP categories.

6 Conclusion and Further Research

We investigated in this work how web scraped product data ca be classified in to the ECOICOP classification schema and how multilingual transfer learning can be applied to transfer results between languages. We demonstrated that zero-shot learning can be very useful, especially in the early phases when no manually labeled data is available. In the future we want to extend this work to further European languages and explore if some language combinations benefit more than others from the transfer from a pretrained single-language classification model and if a multilingual model generalizes for transfer learning. We found the predicted scores for the categories to be a good proxy for the certainty of the model and we expect that the generic framework introduced here can be reused for many different languages by changing only language-specific parts. This would help to focus the manual classification effort for millions of products that needs to be enhanced on a continuous basis. Furthermore, we want to include all ECOICOP categories in a generalized manner.

References

Jacek Białek and Maciej Berkesewicz. 2020. Scanner data in inflation measurement: from raw data to price indices. *arXiv: Applications*.

Piotr Bojanowski, Edouard Grave, Armand Joulin, and Tomas Mikolov. 2017. Enriching word vectors with subword information. *Transactions of the Association for Computational Linguistics*, 5:135–146.

Tolga Bolukbasi, Kai-Wei Chang, James Y Zou, Venkatesh Saligrama, and Adam T Kalai. 2016. Man is to computer programmer as woman is to homemaker? debiasing word embeddings. In *Advances in neural information processing systems*, pages 4349–4357.

Alberto Cavallo and Roberto Rigobon. 2016. The billion prices project: Using online prices for measurement and research. *Journal of Economic Perspectives*, 30(2):151–178.

Alberto Cavallo, Gita Gopinath, Brent Neiman, and Jenny Tang. 2019. Tariff passthrough at the border and at the store: evidence from us trade policy. Technical report, National Bureau of Economic Research.

Jindong Chen, Yizhou Hu, Jingping Liu, Yanghua Xiao, and Haiyun Jiang. 2019. Deep short text classification with knowledge powered attention. In *Proceedings of the AAAI Conference on Artificial Intelligence*, volume 33, pages 6252–6259.

Akiko Eriguchi, Melvin Johnson, Orhan Firat, Hideto Kazawa, and Wolfgang Macherey. 2018. Zero-shot cross-lingual classification using multilingual neural machine translation. *arXiv preprint arXiv:1809.04686*.

European Union. 2016. Regulation (eu) 2016/792 of the european parliament and of the council of 11 may 2016 on harmonised indices of consumer prices and the house price index, and repealing council regulation (ec) no 2494/95. *Official Journal of the European Union*, 59(24 May).

Eurostat. 2020. Faq - eurostat. `https://ec.europa.eu/eurostat/web/hicp/faq`. (Accessed on 06/12/2020).

Jonas Gehring, Michael Auli, David Grangier, Denis Yarats, and Yann N Dauphin. 2017. Convolutional sequence to sequence learning. *arXiv preprint arXiv:1705.03122*.

Sepp Hochreiter and Jürgen Schmidhuber. 1997. Long short-term memory. *Neural computation*, 9:1735–80, 12.

Melvin Johnson, Mike Schuster, Quoc V Le, Maxim Krikun, Yonghui Wu, Zhifeng Chen, Nikhil Thorat, Fernanda Viégas, Martin Wattenberg, Greg Corrado, et al. 2017. Google's multilingual neural machine translation system: Enabling zero-shot translation. *Transactions of the Association for Computational Linguistics*, 5:339–351.

Armand Joulin, Piotr Bojanowski, Tomas Mikolov, Hervé Jégou, and Edouard Grave. 2018. Loss in translation: Learning bilingual word mapping with a retrieval criterion. *arXiv preprint arXiv:1804.07745*.

Efsun Sarioglu Kayi, Vishal Anand, and Smaranda Muresan. 2020. Multiseg: Parallel data and subword information for learning bilingual embeddings in low resource scenarios. In *Proceedings of the 1st Joint Workshop on Spoken Language Technologies for Under-resourced languages (SLTU) and Collaboration and Computing for Under-Resourced Languages (CCURL)*, pages 97–105.

Yoon Kim. 2014. Convolutional neural networks for sentence classification. In *Proceedings of the 2014 Conference on Empirical Methods in Natural Language Processing (EMNLP)*, pages 1746–1751, Doha, Qatar, October. Association for Computational Linguistics.

Alexandre Klementiev, Ivan Titov, and Binod Bhattarai. 2012. Inducing crosslingual distributed representations of words. In *Proceedings of COLING 2012*, pages 1459–1474, Mumbai, India, December. The COLING 2012 Organizing Committee.

Timo Koskimäki and Mari Ylä-Jarkko. 2003. Segmented markets and cpi elementary classifications. In *seventh meeting of the International working group on price indices, Paris*, pages 27–29.

Austin C Kozlowski, Matt Taddy, and James A Evans. 2019. The geometry of culture: Analyzing the meanings of class through word embeddings. *American Sociological Review*, 84(5):905–949.

Alex Krizhevsky, Ilya Sutskever, and Geoffrey E Hinton. 2012. Imagenet classification with deep convolutional neural networks. In *Advances in neural information processing systems*, pages 1097–1105.

Ji Young Lee and Franck Dernoncourt. 2016. Sequential short-text classification with recurrent and convolutional neural networks. *arXiv preprint arXiv:1603.03827*.

Paweł Macias and Damian Stelmasiak. 2019. Food inflation nowcasting with web scraped data. Technical report.

Hazel Martindale, Edward Rowland, and Tanya Flower. 2019. Semi-supervised machine learning with word embedding for classification in price statistics. In *16th Meeting of the International Working Group on Price Indices*, Rio de Janeiro, Brazil.

Tomas Mikolov, Quoc V Le, and Ilya Sutskever. 2013. Exploiting similarities among languages for machine translation. *arXiv preprint arXiv:1309.4168*.

Ben Powell, Guy Nason, Duncan Elliott, Matthew Mayhew, Jennifer Davies, and Joe Winton. 2018. Tracking and modelling prices using web-scraped price microdata: towards automated daily consumer price index forecasting. *Journal of the Royal Statistical Society: Series A (Statistics in Society)*, 181(3):737–756.

Radim Řehůřek and Petr Sojka. 2010. Software Framework for Topic Modelling with Large Corpora. In *Proceedings of the LREC 2010 Workshop on New Challenges for NLP Frameworks*, pages 45–50, Valletta, Malta, May. ELRA.

Tulika Saha, Sriparna Saha, and Pushpak Bhattacharyya. 2019. Tweet act classification: A deep learning based classifier for recognizing speech acts in twitter. In *2019 International Joint Conference on Neural Networks (IJCNN)*, pages 1–8. IEEE.

Seungwan Seo, Czangyeob Kim, Haedong Kim, Kyounghyun Mo, and Pilsung Kang. 2020. Comparative study of deep learning-based sentiment classification. *IEEE Access*, 8:6861–6875.

Burr Settles. 2009. Active learning literature survey. Computer Sciences Technical Report 1648, University of Wisconsin–Madison.

Jin Wang, Zhongyuan Wang, Dawei Zhang, and Jun Yan. 2017. Combining knowledge with deep convolutional neural networks for short text classification. In *IJCAI*, volume 350.

Shiyao Wang, Minlie Huang, and Zhidong Deng. 2018. Densely connected cnn with multi-scale feature attention for text classification. In *IJCAI*, pages 4468–4474.

Will Y Zou, Richard Socher, Daniel Cer, and Christopher D Manning. 2013. Bilingual word embeddings for phrase-based machine translation. In *Proceedings of the 2013 Conference on Empirical Methods in Natural Language Processing*, pages 1393–1398.

Interrupt me Politely: Recommending Products and Services by Joining Human Conversation

Boris Galitsky
Oracle Inc, USA
Boris.galitsky@oracle.com

Dmitry Ilvovsky
HSE University, Moscow, Russia
dilvovsky@hse.ru

Abstract

We propose a novel way of conversational recommendation, where instead of asking questions to the user to acquire their preferences; the recommender tracks their conversation with other people, including customer support agents (CSA), and joins the conversation only when it is time to introduce a recommendation. Building a recommender that joins a human conversation (RJC), we propose information extraction, discourse and argumentation analyses, as well as dialogue management techniques to compute a recommendation for a product and service that is needed by the customer, as inferred from the conversation. A special case of such conversations is considered where the customer raises his problem with CSA in an attempt to resolve it, along with receiving a recommendation for a product with features addressing this problem. We evaluate performance of RJC is in a number of human-human and human-chat bot dialogues, and demonstrate that RJC is an efficient and less intrusive way to provide high relevance and persuasive recommendations.

1 Introduction

Due to the popularity of texting and messaging, in combination with a recent advancement of deep learning technologies, a conversation-based recommendation has become an emerging platform for advertising. While modern conversation platforms offer basic conversation capabilities such as natural language understanding, entity extraction and simple dialogue management, there are still challenges in developing practical applications to support complex use cases such as recommendation, relying on dialogue systems (Thompson et al 2004; Christakopoulou et al., 2016; Sun and Zhang, 2018).

Over the last 2 or 3 years, much more precise and powerful recommendation algorithms have been created which are better more effectively assessing users' tastes, and predicting any relevant information that would be of interest to them. Most of these approaches rely on machine learning-based collaborative techniques, and do not take into account the huge amount of knowledge, both structured and non-structured, such as prior user utterances in a dialogue, which describe the domain of interest for the recommendation engine (Anelli et al., 2018).

A conversational advertising agent could have much more commercial potential in comparison with a conventional advertising such as random insertion in a sequence of conversation, as provided by a social advertising network like Facebook. But research on this topic is very limited and existing solutions are either based on single round conventional search or a traditional multi round dialog system. Web portals such as Amazon, eBay, JD, Alibaba and others usually only utilize user inputs in the current session, ignoring users' long term preferences, or just perform slot-filling, obtaining the parameters of interest from the user explicitly (Sun and Zhang, 2018). Moreover, most of such systems behave very differently from a human when they asked for a recommendation (Galitsky, 2019; Christakopoulou et al., 2016). Humans can quickly establish preferences when asked to make a recommendation for someone they do not know.

Although RJC is an effective and efficient means of advertising and marketing, nowadays even a conventional advertisement can be significantly improved by simple filters, like preventing ads for poorly-rated products.

Proceedings of the Workshop on Natural Language Processing in E-Commerce (EComNLP), pages 32–42
Barcelona, Spain (Online), Dec 12, 2020.

In this paper, we formulate a broader advertising and recommendation problem learning user preferences implicitly from the previous utterances in an arbitrary problem-solving conversation, not just by asking explicitly about user preferences. We introduce a recommendation by joining a conversation (RJC), a special case of conversational advertisement with a focus on assisting with solving a current customer problem or need being communicated. In RJC scenarios, customers are expected to be fully aware of how and why a product or service being recommended would solve their issues.

We consider two types of RJC scenarios:

- User - Human CSA dialogue, where an automated advertisement agent tracks it and inserts its utterances with recommendation

- User – Chat bot CS, where an automated advertisement agents and a chat bot is the same entity resolving a customer problem and providing product/service recommendation at the same time.

2 Sample Dialogues with Recommendations

One of the main requirement for the advertising in the course of CS dialogue is that the relation to the product the user experiences problem with must be obvious, as well as the benefits to the user of relying on this new recommended product to overcome this problem.

We start with an example of casual conversation and demonstrate how an advertising utterance can naturally appear. *Example 1:*

```
Mike: Hey, what's up, dude?
Peter: Not much. I am looking for a DVD to rent but I am fed up
with all these. Have seen most of them already
Mike: Anything worth seeing at the movie theater?
Peter: Nah. Just kids movies, sci-fi and cheesy romantic come-
dies.
RJC-agent: If you are looking for something new you should come
to a meeting of the New Age Alternative Films Club
Peter: What is that?
RJC-agent: the New Age Alternative Films Club gets together eve-
ry other week and screens the type of films you cannot go at a
regular movie theater
```

An utterance of RJC agent can be followed by additional factual questions RJC should be able to answer. *Example 2:*

```
Agent: It's a good day today at Bank of Wealth, my name is
Heather. How can I help you?
Customer: I would like to know my remaining money in my account.
Agent: I'll be glad to help you. May I please get your Bank Ac-
count number and the Name on the Account?
Customer: Sure, it's Tracy Q. Randall, account number is ****.
Agent: Thank you, let me just check on it. Ok, can you, please,
verify the last four numbers of your social security ID.
Customer: It is ****.
Agent: You still have 84 thousand and 65 cents. Is there any-
thing else that I could assist you with?
Customer: Yes, if I transfer it to my bank account in Lloyds of
London, how long will it take?
Agent: If we do the transaction over the phone or online, our
team will still contact you for verification prior sending your
money to a different bank.
RJC-agent: Open Account in Morgan Chase and use Zelle QuickPay
to quickly transfer money to your friends and partners abroad
```

An applicability of the proposed recommendation setting can go beyond CS scenarios. Daily conversations are rich in emotion. By expressing emotions, people show their mutual respect, empathy and understanding to each other, and thus improve the relationships (Li et al., 2017). ***Example 3:***

```
Riley: Are you still auditioning for that skin cream commercial?
Katie: That just so happens to be the 'in thing'. Does not every
aspiring actress start off in a commercial?
Riley: I take it you did not get the part of that 'Life and
Death' sitcom?
Katie: They did not even let me audition
RJC-agent: Have you thought about taking acting lessons? Have
you heard about Beverly Hills Playhouse - Acting Classes Los An-
geles?
```

3   Computing Recommendation for a Dialogue

In a regular recommendation / advertisement scenario, any popular product or the one meeting the user preferences is considered to be appropriate. Conversely, in the RJC scenario a recommended product or service must be related to the product which is the main entity of the problem being resolved. We show the cases of typical customer problems in various domains:

1) A customer does not maintain a positive balance carefully and now wants to avoid NSF in the future.

2) A traveler with a pet finds himself in a hotel that does not allow dogs.

3) A traveler got a non-changeable air ticket and now wants to change the flight.

In most of these cases (Table 1) the features of products and services were disclosed to customers but they did not pay enough attention. These customers contact CS and complain. This is a good time to recommend an alternative product or an addition to a service.

Subject of the problem	Focus of a conversation	Product to recommend	Recommended feature	Search query
Checking account	No overdraft protection	Saving account	Linked with checking for overdraft protection	X for checking account with overdraft protection
Hotel @ <location>	No dogs allowed	Apartment	Dog friendly	Dog friendly apartment X @ <location>
Flight to <destination>	Ticket is not changeable	Flight insured for change of plans	Coverage for change of plans / air ticket change	Travel insurance for flight by X to <destination>
Camping tent of <brand>	Hard to pitch	Self-pitching tent	Tube frames allowing for self-pitching	Camping tent of <brand> X with self-pitching
Auto insurance from X	Does not cover roadside assistance	Additional coverage	Covering roadside assistance	Additional coverage X with roadside assistance

Table 1. Examples of seed and recommended products

The queries have a placeholder **X** for product/service name such as account type, accommodation name, air travel company, etc. The role of this placeholder in a query is to assure the respective entity type does occur in an acceptable search result.

Processing steps in the RJC component are the following:

1) Extract noun phrases from utterance.

2) Identify an entity which is a seed product or service.

3) Relying on the ontology, identify a product attribute. Ontology is required to identify a parameter/feature of the seed entity that is a focus of a conversation with a CS. Relations in ontology are *Part-*

of, Type-of, Same-as, Instance-of, Defines, Defined-by and others (Hoffman, 2015). A feature of a product is connected with this product by *Part-of, Type-of* or *Instance-of*.

4) Relying on ontology, form a search query against an index of products with desired attribute.

5) Accumulate for further processing the list of identified product candidates to be recommended.

4   How to make Recommendation more Persuasive?

A number of studies including (Berkovsky et al., 2012) demonstrated that explanation and persuasion are two important characteristics for convincing users to follow the recommendations. ***Example 4:***

```
Customer: You charged me unfair NSF but I maintained a positive
balance on my account.
Agent: We have to charge NSF to maintain our income, so you
should maintain minimum balance.
Good RJC-Agent: I recommend you a product such that you avoid a
negative balance. You should get our product linked checking-
saving account with overdraft protection, so that NSF never hap-
pens again.
Marginally Relevant but unpersuasive-Agent: Open new account at
Base Bank. High Yield interest rates. Open within next week and
get a free checking.
Irrelevant-Agent: Earn income working from home. No training is
necessary. Start making money right now.
Relevant but unpersuasive Agent: Get an overdraft protection.
Link a saving account with your checking one.
```

We use a traditional advertisement format for the irrelevant and unpersuasive examples. A good example is a free-format text that includes a recommendation as well as its argumentative back up, an explanation why this product would solve a customer problem, as described in dialogue (Ex. 4). Negative examples rely on imperative form of verbs that is heavily used in conventional advertisement.

To be a good recommendation, it needs to relate to the seed product and to its features and attributes that are the subjects of the conversation. In addition, discourse structure of the recommendation text matters (Fig. 2).

Discourse tree representation (RST, Mann and Thompson, 1988) for a recommendation allows to judge on its quality and can be constructed automatically (Joty et.al, 2015). If rhetorical relations of *Explanation, Cause, Enablement* are recognized in recommendation text (Galitsky and Ilvovsky, 2019) then there is a higher chance that this recommendation is reasonable, persuasive and well argued.

```
cause
   explanation
      TEXT: I recommend you a product,
      TEXT: to avoid a negative balance.
   enablement
      TEXT: Therefore, you should get our product "linked check-
ing-saving account with overdraft protection''
      TEXT: so that NSF never happens again.
```

Fig. 2. Discourse Tree for a good answer (underlined in Ex. 4)

Recommendation with a discourse tree that contains only default rhetorical relations such as *Elaboration* and *Join* would not be as good. Moreover, discourse representation of the recommendation must match in terms of argumentation that of the problem description of the product by customer. A generalized example of a proper correlation between the previous utterances about the seed product P and recommendation R is shown in ***Example 5:***

```
Customer: there is a problem with feature F of product P
Agent: It can (or cannot be fixed) by doing (this and that) with
F of P
Customer: No you still cannot fix problem of P …
```

```
RJC-agent:Product R will fix this problem with F of P since R's
feature RF covers F
```

To assure a recommendation makes sense to a user, it needs to be backed up by an argument. To find a textual recommendation that will be perceived by the user, this recommendation should form a well backed up claim where the utterances in the dialogue are premises.

For argumentation support in RJC we employ a modified Toulmin's model (Toulmin, 1958) which contains five argument components, namely: *claim, premise, backing, rebuttal, and refutation.*

In this model any arbitrary token span can be labeled with an argument component; the components do not overlap. All components are optional (they do not have to be present in the argument) except the claim, which is either explicit or implicit. If a token span is not labeled by any argument component, it is not considered as a part of the argument. Relations from this model can be constructed automatically using extended discourse tree representation (Galitsky et al., 2018).

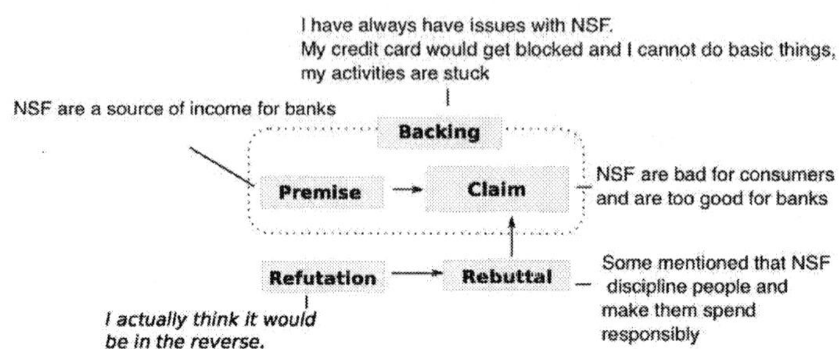

Fig. 3. Toulmin's model and its instance in the domain of non-sufficient fund fees (NSF)

Example of this model built for the sample dialogue on NSF is shown on Fig. 3. The arrows show relations between argument components; the relations are implicit and inherent in the model.

In case of the pair of products *P* and *RP*, a recommendation for RP must be *supported* by the customers' expression of their needs and problems in *P*.

5   Dialogue Management in RJC Agent

Once a recommendation utterance is delivered, the user may choose to continue conversation with Ad-agent. Then the following algorithm is applied (Algorithm 1).

Algorithm 1

Input: Recommendations = top-5 recommendations, Profile = user preferences, Graph = graph representation of user preferences, items, entities, properties
Output: conversation
1: Profile ← Profile + new preferences (items, entities, properties);
2: Recommendations ← PageRank (Graph, Profile); Show Recommendations;
3: **while** User does not accept Recommendations do
4: Feedback ← User feedback;
5: Refine(Feedback);
6: Recommendations ← PageRank (Graph, Profile); Show Recommendations;
7: End

To build a conversational grammar for dialogue management, we introduce the notion of adjacency-pair, sequences of two utterances that are adjacent (not separated by an insertion sequence), produced by different speakers and ordered as a first ("initiative") and a second ("response") part.

Both parts should also belong to a certain type, so that a particular initiative requires a certain type or range of types of the response.

Adjacency-pairs are *question-answer, greeting-greeting,* or *offer-acceptance/decline.* Where there is a range of potential responses to an initiative (as with offer-acceptance/decline), a ranking operates over the options designating one response as preferred (in the sense of normal, more usual) and others as less preferred (Bridge, 2002). Less preferred responses tend to be longer, linguistically more complex. Having produced a first part of a pair, the current speaker must stop speaking and it is expected that the next speaker will produce one of the allowable second parts of the same pair. The second part will often follow immediately. However, there frequently occur insertion sequences. These are sequences of turns that intervene between the first and second parts of a pair; the second part is in a holding pattern during the insertion sequence.

We use Prolog notations for the dialogue grammar: variables are capitalized:

1) **turn(system, [], [(Type, Topic)]) --> initiative(system, Type, Topic).** There are no ongoing pairs. The system starts a new pair.

2) **turn(user, [(Type, Topic) | Rest], Rest) --> response(user, Type, Topic).** There is at least one ongoing pair. The user provides a response of the same type and on the same topic, thus completing the pair.

3) **turn(system, [(Type, Topic)], [(Type$_1$, Topic$_1$)]) --> response(system, Type, Topic), initiative(system, Type$_1$, Topic$_1$).** There is a single ongoing pair. The system provides a response of the same type and on the same topic and initiates a new pair of a possibly different type and on a possibly different topic.

4) **turn(system, [(Type, Topic), (Type$_1$, Topic) | Rest], [(Type1, Topic) | Rest]) --> response(system, Type, Topic), initiative(system, Type$_1$, Topic).** There are at least two ongoing pairs on the same topic. The dialogue must have entered an insertion sequence. The system provides a response to complete the most recent pair and reminds the user of the ongoing pair. The grammar achieves this by requiring that the system initiate a new pair of the same type and topic as the ongoing one but it does not push it onto the stack of ongoing pairs, which remains unchanged.

5) **turn(user, [(Type, Topic) | _], [(Type$_1$, Topic$_1$)]) --> response(user, Type, Topic), initiative(user, Type$_1$, Topic$_1$).** There is at least one ongoing pair. The user provides a response to complete the pair and initiates a new pair. This aborts any other ongoing pairs so the stack contains only the new pair.

6) **turn(user, [(_, Topic) | _], [(Type$_1$, Topic$_1$)]) --> initiative(user, Type$_1$, Topic$_1$), {Topic \= Topic$_1$}.** There is at least one ongoing pair. The user aborts it and initiates something new. This is not an insertion sequence because the topic is different.

7) **turn(user, [(Type, Topic) | Rest], [(Type$_1$, Topic), (Type, Topic) | Rest]) --> initiative(user, Type1, Topic).** There is at least one ongoing pair. The user begins an insertion sequence by not responding to the ongoing pair but by initiating a new pair on the same topic. Both pairs are now on the stack.

The grammar restricts contributions that the system can make to the dialogue. In particular, the system cannot abort pairs: rules 5 and 6 apply only to the user. We feel that it is inappropriate for the system to ignore user initiatives.

6   System Architecture

High-level system architecture of RJC is shown in Fig. 3. The system tracks the dialogue and attempt to identify a moment where the customer is about to give up on the CSA problem resolution, or is still unhappy after the problem is solved. This tracking is done based on emotional profile and sentiment profile (Galitsky, 2019). Once such utterance is identified, RJC finds a noun phrase in it, and then identifies a product name together with its feature. Entity extraction is done by Stanford NLP augmented by the product-specific entity rules and product-specific lookup such as eBay product catalogue. Product-related named entities could also be verified by consulting eBay product search API.

Then a search query from the formed product name and its feature is formed, and a search is launched. The search results form a list of candidates, which are filtered based on the proper argumentation and discourse coordination requirements. This filtering is implemented via argument mining and reasoning techniques. They verify that the recommendation as a claim is logically supported by the previous customer utterance and therefore this recommendation would be convincing for the customer. Rhetorical agreement (Galitsky, 2017) is verified based on coordination between the discourse trees of previous customer utterances and the discourse tree of the candidate recommendation text.

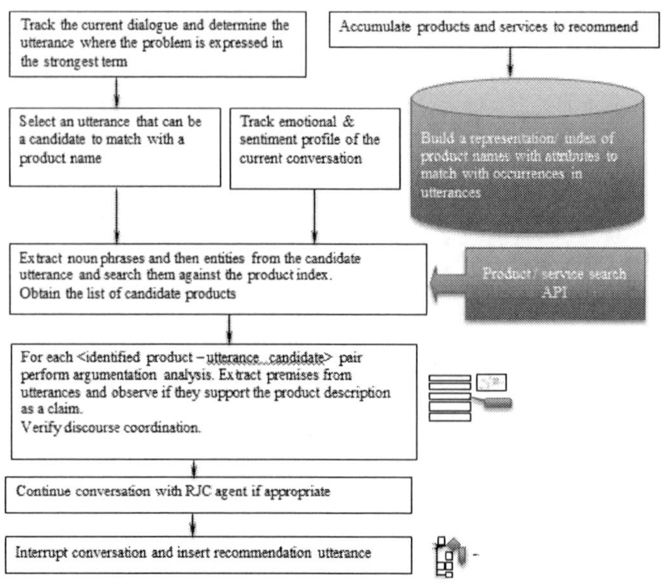

Fig.3. High level system architecture

7 Evaluation

7.1 Datasets

Source type	#	Origin of the data	Recommended source
Finance	2200	my3cents.com bankrate.com	Search of Bloomberg, Fidelity, Bankrate for financial products
Auto repair	9300	2carpros.com	Web search for services
Sports shopping	2740	REI and L.L.Bean data from RichRelevance.com	Internal API for product search
Home products shopping	3100	Walmart, HD Supply, OfficeDepot data from RichRelevance.com	eBay product search API
Home-related services		Yelp reviews	Yelp API
Travel	2430	zicasso.com/travel-reviews, tripadvisor.com reviews Airline forums on TripAdvisor.com	Tripadvisor.com
Daily dialogues	2000	(Li et al., 2018)	Yelp API
Genuine human dialogues	2000	(Li et al., 2018); ENRON email thread; Reddit discourse dataset (Logacheva et al., 2018)	Yelp API, eBay product search, Tripadvisor.com, Bing Forum search, Bing Web search
Constructed from blogs, etc.	5200	2carpros.com; immihelp.com; blog.feedspot.com; librarything.com/groups	

Table 2. Characteristics of the data sources

We use various source of dialogues: a) Conversational data sets; b) Data scraped from online forums; c) Cached search results from specific APIs. For scraped and indexed data we use our own search for products, and for web data we either use APIs of a particular source or search this source via Bing API.

We obtain human-human dialogues from Customer Complaints and Car Repair datasets. For the first dataset, we obtain recommendations online from websites like www.bankrate.com and www.bloomberg.com. We obtain recommendation sources from Yelp on restaurants and services such as repair and tuition. For book recommendations we used Amazon/LibraryThing (A/LT) dataset available at www.librarything.com/groups. For blogs and forums which can potentially be subject to RJC we relied on www.2carpros.com, www.immihelp.com, www.talkhealthpartnership.com and blog.feedspot.com.

To get closer to the CSA conversation setting, we selected Relational Strategies in Customer Service Dataset that is collection of travel-related customer service data from four sources. The conversation logs of three commercial customer service IVAs and the Airline forums on TripAdvisor.com. For a special case of conversations related to overall product opinion we employ the Customer Support on Twitter dataset. It includes over 3 million tweets and replies from the biggest brands on Twitter. The datasets to evaluate RJC are enumerated in Table 2.

The Reddit discourse dataset (Zhang et al., 2017) is manually annotated with dialog-acts via crowd sourcing. The dialogue acts comprise of answer, question, humor, agreement, disagreement, appreciation, negative reaction, elaboration, and announcement. It contains conversations from around 9000 randomly sampled Reddit threads with over 100000 comments and an average of 12 turns per thread.

7.2   Evaluation Results

Source type	Correct dialogue turn	Entity extraction from dialogue	Product entity is properly matched	Acceptable argumentation	Proper discourse	Overall meaningfulness
Finance	91.3	94.5	91.2	73.2	79.4	72.9
Auto repair	88.4	96.0	92.6	78.1	84.2	74.3
Sports shopping	89.6	92.9	90.4	76.0	82.3	71.4
Home products shopping	90.3	92.1	94.7	78.3	80.6	72.7
Home-related services	89.3	93.7	91.7	72.7	76.5	73.3
Travel	90.8	92.7	93.6	73.9	82.4	75.2
Daily Dialogues	88.4	89.3	92.0	71.9	80.7	72.6
Genuine human dialogues	89.3	91.6	88.3	67.3	74.2	68.2
Constructed from blogs, etc.	90.4	92.7	90.7	70.8	73.7	71.4

Table 3. Accuracy of the RJC components

Recommendation by joining a conversation turns out to have a high overall relevance and appropriateness to needs of customers (right column in Table 3). The accuracy range of 68-74% shows that three quarters of recommendations should not cause user irritation and instead encourage a user to buy a product, which would address a problem raised in conversation. Although we do not assess an actual conversion rate of RJC one can see that this form of recommendation and advertisement is least intrusive and has the highest instant relevance in comparison with other conversational recommendation means. Two greyed bottom rows in Table 3 show the datasets where we access the applicability of dialogue generation in comparison with genuine dialogues.

Accuracies of each component vary from domain to domain by less than 10% due to different linguistic and logical complexity of dialogues, product searches and argumentation analysis. Bottom greyed three rows show that genuine human dialogues are a bit more complex than the artificial ones obtained from documents (although the latter has more formal, professional language).

8   Related Work

In the course of a customer support dialogue, recommendation and advertisement need to be very relevant to customer needs and should assist in problem resolution in the way obvious to this user. In a conventional conversational recommendation, the system first gets information from the user about his needs and preferences and recommends a product after that. To manage such a dialogue in an arbitrary domain, nontrivial dialogue management efforts are required (Galitsky and Ilvovsky, 2017, 2019; Narducci et al., 2018, Sun and Zhang, 2018; Galitsky, 2019). Moreover, a user needs to be very patient and perform a routine activity of specifying his preferences. Neither of these is required in RJC setting.

Argument mining techniques make it possible to capture the underlying motivations consumers express in reviews. Villalba and Saint-Dizier (2012) describe how argument detection can occur on the TextCoop platform. Taking the dialogical perspective, Cabrio and Villata (2012) built upon an argumentation framework proposed by Dung (1995) which models arguments within a graph structure and provides a reasoning mechanism for resolving accepted arguments.

A number of studies investigated persuasiveness in the sense that is applied to advertising. Schlosser (2011) investigated persuasiveness of online reviews and concluded that presenting two sides is not always more helpful and can even be less persuasive than presenting one side. Miceli et al. (2006) describe a computational model that attempts to integrate emotional and non-emotional persuasion. Bernard et al. (2012) investigate children's perception of discourse connectives to link statements in arguments and found out that 4-years-old and adults are sensitive to the connectives.

Advertising in the course of dialogue is connected with dialogue marketing that is the generic term for all marketing activities in which media is used with the intention of establishing an interactive relationship with individuals. The aim is to initiate an individual, measurable response from the recipient (Jaffe, 2008). A relationship dialogue is a process of reasoning together in order for two or more parties to develop a common knowledge platform (Grönroos, 2000). Relationship marketing knowledge platform enables a supplier to create additional value for its customers on top of the value of the goods which are exchanged in the relationship. There have been many works emphasizing the importance of interactivity in recommenders so that the user has more active role over the recommendations. It includes critique-based recommendations (Chen and Pu, 2012), constraint-based (Felfernig et al., 2011), dialogue, utility-based recommenders. However, these studies employ a prior modeling of the items' features, preventing the flexibility in adaptation to different recommendation domains.

9   Paper Summary and Conclusion

We observe that it was necessary to track sentiments and the strength of emotion in the user-CSA conversation. When sentiment is not too negative and emotion is not too strong it might be too early to induce a recommendation since there is a chance that the conflict is resolved among the humans. If the sentiment and emotions are too negative, it is time for a recommender to intervene. This way we achieve timeliness, less intrusiveness and overall relevance of RJC recommendation. The goal of our RJC Dialogue Manager is to "interrupt politely". We believe that in general, a sponsored post does not have to be necessarily irrelevant; a broader match with a catalog of sponsor products needs to be implemented so that every user can get a recommendation according to her specific interests and desires, expressed in communication with peers. Also, the proposed algorithm would not deliver annoying repetitive recommendations as most advertisers and industrial recommender systems do.

We summarize this paper by enumerating the observed features of RJC:
1) Recommendation by joining a conversation turns out to have a high overall relevance and appropriateness to the needs of customers;
2) The accuracy range of 68-74% shows that at least 0.75 of recommendations should not cause user irritation and instead encourage a user to buy a recommended product;
3) In most cases the recommended products and services indeed address a customer problem raised in conversation;
4) Explainable AI – compliant: it is clear why this product is needed;
5) This form of recommendation and advertisement is least intrusive as the RJC utterance can be ignored.

One of the tasks of a future study is to evaluate an actual convergence rate of the RJC advertisement mode.

Acknowledgements

The article was prepared within the framework of the HSE University Basic Research Program and funded by the Russian Academic Excellence Project '5-100'.

Reference

Anelli VW, Pierpaolo Basile, Derek Bridge, Tommaso Di Noia, Pasquale Lops, Cataldo Musto, Fedelucio Nar-duc-ci, and Zanker M (2018) Knowledge-aware and conver-sational recommender systems. 12th ACM Conference on Recommender Systems (RecSys '18). ACM, New York, NY, USA, 521-522

Berkovsky S, Jill Freyne, and Harri Oinas-Kukkonen (2012) Influencing individually: fusing personalization and per-suasion. ACM Transactions on Interactive Intelligent Systems (TiiS), 2(2):9.

Bernard S, Hugo Mercier, and Fabrice Clément (2012) The power of well-connected arguments: early sensitivity to the connective because. Journal of experimental child psychology, 111(1):128–35.

Bridge D (2002) Towards Conversational Recommender Systems: A Dialogue Grammar Approach. Proceedings of the Workshop in Mixed-Initiative Case-Based Reasoning, Workshop Program at the Sixth European Conference in Case-Based Reasoning, 9-22.

Cabrio E and Serena Villata (2013) A natural language bi-polar argumentation approach to support users in online debate interactions. Argument & Computation, 4(3):209–230.

Chen L and P. Pu (2012) Critiquing-based recommenders: survey and emerging trends. In User Modeling and User-Adapted Interaction, 22(1-2):125–150.

Christakopoulou K, Filip Radlinski, and Katja Hofmann (2016) Towards Conversational Recommender Systems. 22nd ACM SIGKDD International Conference on Knowledge Discovery and Data Mining (KDD '16). ACM, New York, NY, USA, 815-824.

Dung P-M (1995) On the acceptability of arguments and its fundamental role in nonmonotonic reasoning, logic pro-gramming and n-person games. Artificial Intelligence, 77(2):321 – 357.

Felfernig A, G. Friedrich, D. Jannach and M. Zanker (2011) Developing Constraint-based Recommenders. In Recommender systems handbook, 187–212.

Galitsky B (2017) Discovering Rhetorical Agreement between a Request and Response. Dialogue and Discourse.

Galitsky B (2019) Developing Enterprise Chatbots Springer, Cham, Switzerland.

Galitsky B and Ilvovsky D (2017) Chatbot with a discourse structure-driven dialogue management. EACL System Demonstrations.

Galitsky B and Ilvovsky D. (2018) Detecting logical argumentation in text via communicative discourse tree. JETAI.

Galitsky B, Ilvovsky D (2019) On a Chatbot Conducting a Virtual Dialogue in Financial Domain. Proceedings of the First Workshop on Financial Technology and Natural Language Processing.

Grönroos C (2000) Creating a Relationship Dialogue: Communication, Interaction and Value. The Marketing Review, V1, N1, pp. 5-14(10).

Hoffman C (2019) Financial Report Ontology. http://www.xbrlsite.com/2015/fro/.

Jaffe J (2008) Join the Conversation: How to Engage Marketing-Weary Consumers with the Power of Community, Dialogue, and Partnership John Wiley & Sons. New Jer-sey US.

Li Y, Hui Su, Xiaoyu Shen, Wenjie Li, Ziqiang Cao, and Shuzi Niu (2017) DailyDialog: A Manually Labelled Multi-turn Dialogue Dataset. IJCNLP.

Lippi M and Torroni P (2016) Argument mining from speech: Detecting claims in political debates. In AAAI, 2979–2985.

Logacheva V., Burtsev M., Malykh V., Polulyakh V., Se-liverstov A. (2018) ConvAI Dataset of Topic-Oriented Human-to-Chatbot Dialogues. NIPS '17 Competition: Building Intelligent Systems. The Springer Series on Challenges in Machine Learning. Springer, Cham

Mann, William and Sandra Thompson. (1988) Rhetorical structure theory: Towards a functional theory of text organization. Text-Interdisciplinary Journal for the Study of Discourse, 8(3):243–281.

Miceli M, Fiorella de Rosis, and Isabella Poggi. (2006) Emotional and non-emotional persuasion. Applied Artificial Intelligence, 20(10):849–879.

Mochales R and Moens M-F (2011) Argumentation mining. Artificial Intelligence and Law, 19(1):1–22.

Narducci F., de Gemmis M., Lops P., Semeraro G. (2018) Improving the User Experience with a Conversational Recommender System. In: AI*IA 2018 – Advances in Artificial Intelligence. AI*IA 2018. Lecture Notes in Computer Science, vol 11298. Springer, Cham.

Schlosser A E. (2011) Can including pros and cons increase the helpfulness and persuasiveness of online reviews? The interactive effects of ratings and arguments. Journal of Consumer Psychology, 21(3):226–239.

Shafiq Joty, Giuseppe Carenini, Raymond T. Ng. (2015) CODRA: A Novel Discriminative Framework for Rhetorical Analysis. Computational Linguistics 41:3, 385-435.

Sun Y and Zhang Y (2018) Conversational Recommender System. SIGIR '18 The 41st International ACM SIGIR Conference on Research & Development in Information Retrieval, 235-244 Ann Arbor, MI, USA.

Thompson CA, Mehmet H. Göker, and Pat Langley (2004) A personalized system for conversational recommendations. J. Artif. Int. Res. 21-1 , 393-428.

Toulmin, S. The Uses of Argument. Cambridge At the University Press, 1958.

Villalba MPG and Patrick Saint-Dizier P (2012) A framework to extract arguments in opinion texts. IJCINI, 6(3):62–87.

Benchmarking Automated Review Response Generation
for the Hospitality Domain

Tannon Kew, Michael Amsler, Sarah Ebling
Department of Computational Linguistics, University of Zurich
`{kew, mamsler, ebling}@cl.uzh.ch`

Abstract

Online customer reviews are of growing importance for many businesses in the hospitality industry, particularly restaurants and hotels. Managerial responses to such reviews provide businesses with the opportunity to influence the public discourse and to attain improved ratings over time. However, responding to each and every review is a time-consuming endeavour. Therefore, we investigate automatic generation of review responses in the hospitality domain for two languages, English and German.

We apply an existing system, originally proposed for review response generation for smartphone apps. This approach employs an extended neural network sequence-to-sequence architecture and performs well in the original domain. However, as shown through our experiments, when applied to a new domain, such as hospitality, performance drops considerably. Therefore, we analyse potential causes for the differences in performance and provide evidence to suggest that review response generation in the hospitality domain is a more challenging task and thus requires further study and additional domain adaptation techniques.

1 Introduction

Online customer reviews play a significant role in e-commerce and specifically in the tourism and hospitality industry. Websites such as TripAdvisor, Booking.com and Yelp offer customers the opportunity to share their experiences in the form of reviews relating to restaurants, cafés, hotels and other business types. To date, TripAdvisor boasts more than 860 million customer reviews and opinions worldwide[1].

While these reviews serve as an important point of reference for potential customers who value and rely on electronic word-of-mouth recommendations (Litvin et al., 2008), it has been shown that they also offer businesses an opportunity to influence the public discourse and foster positive customer relations by responding to these reviews appropriately (see Li et al. (2017); Li et al. (2018)). However, given the sheer amount of online reviews, composing these responses is a time-consuming and costly endeavour for any business.

In this paper, we report on automated response generation for hospitality reviews, specifically restaurants and hotels, in both English and German. While a similar task has previously been tackled for product reviews in online stores in Chinese (Zhao et al., 2019) and for smartphone app reviews in English (Gao et al., 2019), the application domain of hospitality reviews is, to the best of our knowledge, novel. In addition, our investigations are applied to two languages, which allows for a valuable idea of how well the approach generalises across languages.

The experiments conducted in this paper leverage the approach proposed by Gao et al. (2019), who extend the basic attentional sequence-to-sequence (seq2seq) neural network (Sutskever et al., 2014; Bahdanau et al., 2015) framework for conditioned text generation. We find that applying the proposed solu-

---

[1] `http://ir.tripadvisor.com/static-files/f81e3d8c-2e18-409f-9ca3-8b3148238257` (last accessed: July 16, 2020)

43

Proceedings of the Workshop on Natural Language Processing in E-Commerce (EComNLP), pages 43–52
Barcelona, Spain (Online), Dec 12, 2020.

tion to hospitality review-response pairs yields a considerable decrease in overall performance compared to the results reported in the original paper in the context of app reviews. An empirical investigation into possible causes for the discrepancy provides evidence to suggest that the task is considerably more challenging in our target domain. Thus, we establish a preliminary baseline for future work on automatic response generation for hospitality reviews.

2 Seq2Seq Review Response Generation

Following previous work (e.g., Gao et al. (2019); Zhao et al. (2019)), we tackle the task of review response generation using the popular seq2seq encoder-decoder framework originally proposed by Sutskever et al. (2014) in the context of neural machine translation (NMT) and successfully applied in a broad range of NLP tasks, including abstractive text summarisation (Rush et al., 2015) and conversational dialogue systems (Vinyals and Le, 2015), among others. The central idea behind the seq2seq framework is as follows: Given an input (source) sequence of length n, $X = \{x_1, \ldots, x_n\}$, and a corresponding output (target) sequence of length m, $Y = \{y_1, \ldots, y_m\}$, we aim to learn a probabilistic mapping function $g(\cdot)$ that allows us to predict a probable target sequence $\hat{Y}$ for a novel source sequence.

2.1 Encoder-Decoder Network

The seq2seq model architecture proposed by Sutskever et al. (2014) comprises two recurrent neural networks (RNNs) which are jointly optimised during training. The first of these reads in the source sequence, *encoding* it into a fixed-length context vector $c \in \mathbb{R}$. The second neural network takes the resulting context vector c as input and effectively *decodes* it, outputting a sequence of target tokens over a number of timesteps $t \in T$ and stopping as soon as a special end-of-sequence token (<EOS>) is produced. Thus, the probability of a target token at timestep t is modelled as

$$\log p(y_t|y_{<t}, c) = g(h'_t, y_{t-1}, c).$$

A major limitation of the original encoder-decoder architecture is the fact that a given source sequence of arbitrary length is represented by the fixed-length context vector c. As a result, the longer the source sequence, the more difficult it becomes to capture and leverage important information from early on in the sequence when generating the target sequence. The attention mechanism, introduced by Bahdanau et al. (2015), helps to alleviate this.

2.2 Attention Mechanism

The attention mechanism provides the decoder access to the entire sequence of encoder hidden states $H = \{h_1, \ldots, h_n\}$ computed on the input sequence rather than only the final hidden state (Bahdanau et al., 2015; Luong et al., 2015). At each decoding timestep t, we dynamically calculate a new context vector c_t that considers the relative importance of elements in the source sequence for generating the current output y_t. This essentially allows the decoder to focus on particular parts of the input sequence during decoding and alleviates the information bottleneck associated with encoding the entire source sequence into a static fixed-length context vector.

2.3 Review Response Generation

While the attentional seq2seq approach described above has been proven to work well for tasks like NMT, it poses several challenges in the context of more free-form text generation. For example, in the context of hospitality reviews, context is typically very limited and responses can range from very generic, one-size-fits-all responses, e.g.,

> "thank you for your kind review . we are glad you enjoyed your visit and hope to see you again very soon !", (1)

to far more personalised responses that address specific topics raised in the review and also include aspects of external factual knowledge that may be relevant for a given response. The response below provides such an example, where information relevant to the input review is set in bold and information that involves external 'world' knowledge is underlined.

> "thanks for your review . we are very happy to hear that you decided to enjoy the **famous cheese fondue and a classic sausage** at our restaurant and , of course , that **you liked it so much** . we 've been serving traditional swiss cuisine since <DIGIT> and are always happy to   (2)
> share our passion for it with our guest . **<NAME> and the whole team were very glad to receive such good feedback** and we are all looking forward to welcoming you back soon ."

Therefore, instead of conditioning solely on the input text, as is done in standard NMT, we ideally want to be able to incorporate additional features that provide relevant contextual knowledge for the response text. To this end, Zhao et al. (2019) exploit a double-encoder-decoder network in which, in addition to the typical source text encoder, a second encoder reads in product-related information from a structured table. At inference time, the decoder has access to both contextual representation vectors by way of a gated multi-source attention mechanism (Arevalo et al., 2017). However, this approach requires appropriate factual tables to be generated for all relevant entities (in our case, restaurants and hotels listed on TripAdvisor), which we do not have access to.

The approach proposed by Gao et al. (2019), on the other hand, relies primarily on information that can be derived from the review text itself or additional metadata that is readily available. The authors identify four main attributes which are provided as additional input to the decoder (dubbed the A-component): (i) the length of the review text, (ii) the review rating, (iii) a sentiment score calculated for the entire review text, and (iv) the category of the app which is the focus of the review.

The motivation for including these attributes is given by Gao et al. (2019) as follows: review length is an important indicator for the length of an output response since it should be appropriate given the length and detail of the review text; the review rating provides valuable information that impacts the response style directly, e.g., expressing an apology given a negative review or expressing thanks given positive feedback (where the lower half of the numeric rating scale is interpreted as corresponding to negative feedback and the upper half to positive feedback, possibly with an ambiguous midpoint in case of odd-numbered scales); the sentiment score attempts to capture the attitude of the reviewer and accounts for instances where the review rating and review text are inconsistent with each other with respect to polarity; and finally, the category attribute provides general contextual information to the decoder since app reviews of different categories typically address different topics.

Additionally, in order to encourage the decoder to produce responses relevant for the input review, the authors exploit an external keyword dictionary developed by Di Sorbo et al. (2016) for the purpose of app review classification. This keyword dictionary (dubbed the K-component) identifies topical words and maps them to one of twelve aspects relevant for app reviews (e.g., 'version', 'GUI', 'pricing', etc.).

The approach proposed by Gao et al. (2019) is relatively straightforward to adapt to our task of review response generation for the hospitality domain in English and German. For this reason, we select it as a basis for our experiments. More details about the implementation of Gao et al. (2019) are given in Section 3.2.

3   Review Response Generation for the Hospitality Domain

3.1   Data

For the purpose of our experiments, we compiled two datasets of review-response pairs for hotels and restaurants published on TripAdvisor, roughly the same size as that of Gao et al.'s app dataset. We collected data in both English and German from nine different countries[2] and performed simple prepro-cessing. Specifically, we used spaCy[3] to mask personal names, toponyms, emails, urls and numbers. For English, texts were converted to lowercase, while for German, nouns and proper nouns, which are

---

[2] Australia, Canada, Ireland, New Zealand, United Kingdom, United States (for English); Austria, Germany, Switzerland (for German).

[3] https://spacy.io/ (last accessed: July 16, 2020)

	Hosp. (en)	Hosp. (de)	Apps
train	320k	259k	280k
valid	40k	32k	14k
test	40k	32k	15k

Table 1: Overview of review-response pair datasets. For comparison, the size of the app review-response dataset by Gao et al. (2019) is also given on the right.

capitalised in standard German, were titlecased and all remaining words lowercased. We also removed duplicate review-response pairs from the dataset before randomly splitting it into training, validation and test sets at a ratio of 80:10:10. Table 1 provides an overview of the datasets.

3.2 Method

The proposed approach incorporates additional features into the encoder-decoder network, namely the A-component and the K-component, introduced in Section 2.3. The implementation by Gao et al. (2019) embeds each of the additional attributes in the A-component into 90-dimensional vectors which are then concatenated with the hidden representation for the source sequence before being passed to the decoder. The K-component is incorporated by concatenating a 20-dimensional vector, indicating whether or not a word represents a certain aspect, with the pre-trained word embeddings. For the most part, we follow the original implementation and use the same hyper-parameters[4]. To ensure comparability, we evaluate the performance of each model after training for three epochs. In this section we describe the few aspects in which our implementation differs from that of Gao et al.'s, namely the choice of pre-trained word embeddings, how we compute the external sentiment analysis attribute features, and how we derive keyword dictionaries for our data set of hospitality review-response pairs in German and English.

Pre-trained Word Embeddings In contrast to the original approach, which uses `GloVe` pre-trained word embeddings (Pennington et al., 2014), we opt for `fastText` pre-trained word embeddings (Grave et al., 2018). The motivation for this is two-fold. Firstly, `fastText` embeddings incorporate subword-level information in the form of character N-gram features. This allows us to derive reasonably well-estimated word embeddings even for out-of-vocabulary (OOV) words, which is crucial given that our corpus consists of user-generated web content, where typos and alternative spellings are frequent. For example, Table 2 shows some examples of commonly found misspellings in our dataset that are largely OOV and thus fail to receive an informative embedding using the pre-trained `GloVe` model. Secondly, pre-trained `fastText` embeddings are readily available for 157 languages[5], including English and German, whereas pre-trained `GloVe` embeddings are only available for English.

Sentiment Analysis As mentioned in Section 2.3, an overall sentiment score is provided to the decoder as part of the A-component. In the original implementation by Gao et al. (2019), the authors make use of SentiStrength (Thelwall et al., 2010) to automatically calculate the polarity of a given review. While SentiStrength is available for both English and German, and has been shown to successfully predict positive or negative sentiment for short social media web texts, where spelling mistakes are frequent, it is primarily only supported on machines running Microsoft Windows. Therefore, we resort to an alternative sentiment analysis tool. VADER (Valence Aware Dictionary for sEntiment Reasoning) (Hutto and Gilbert, 2014) employs a human-validated sentiment lexicon mapping lexical features (e.g., words) to a valence score, indicating its sentiment polarity and intensity. This lexicon is then combined with five general rules that consider grammatical and syntactic features which influence sentiment (e.g., use of punctuation, all-caps and degree modifiers such as 'very'). VADER has been shown to perform well

---

[4]Word embedding size = 100, number of hidden layers = 1, hidden layer size = 200, dropout rate = 0.1 and batch size = 32. Optimisation is performed with Adam (Kingma and Ba, 2017) with initial learning rate = 0.001 and weight decay = 0.00001. Since our texts are more varied (see Section 3.4), we limit the source and target vocabulary size to the 20,000 most frequent words, which is twice the size of the original implementation.

[5]`https://fasttext.cc/docs/en/crawl-vectors.html` (last accessed: July 16, 2020)

Canonical form	Common misspellings
restaurant	resturant (707), restuarant (362), restaraunt (163), restraunt (146), resteraunt (124), restaurent (50), resturaunt (42), restauraunt (28), restauarant (28), restarant (23), ...
accommodation	accomodation (1,130), accomadation (67), accommodation (12), accomdation (12), accommadation (9), accomidation (7), ...

Table 2: Common misspellings found in our corpus. Note, inspecting the two pre-trained embedding models shows that the most common misspellings 'restuarant' and 'accomodation' are indeed represented in the GloVe model, however, both words receive rather low similarity scores to their canonical forms (0.13 and 0.61, respectively). With the pre-trained fastText model, all variants receive similarity scores above 0.33.

across a broad range of domains, and particularly on social media texts (see Hutto and Gilbert (2014)).

While VADER was primarily developed for English, it is extensible and adaptable to other languages since it relies on a lexicon-based approach extended with simple heuristics. Tymann et al. (2019) propose GerVADER, which replaces the standard VADER lexicon with a slightly extended version of the German sentiment lexicon SentiWS (Remus et al., 2010).

It should be noted that GerVADER is shown to perform reasonably well on the classification of positive sentiment texts but performs poorly on negative sentiment texts due to the fact that negations in German often occur after the verb which they modify (e.g., *Ich gehe **niemals** zurück!* ('I go never back!')) as opposed to English, where they usually appear before (e.g., 'I never go back!'). The current version of GerVADER fails to account for such syntactic differences between the two languages and is thus sub-optimal. Nevertheless, we make use of this off-the-shelf tool due to its availability and ease of application in the target domain.

Review Categories   Gao et al. (2019) make use of the category attribute feature to distinguish reviews according to the genre of the relevant app. Since we do not have such fine-grained categories in our dataset, we simply distinguish between whether the review pertains to a hotel or a restaurant. We note, however, that a more fine-grained distinction regarding the nature of an establishment (e.g., 'take-away', 'fine-dining', 'coffee shop', etc. for restaurants) could be more beneficial for ensuring that the model learns relevant patterns from review-response examples.

Keyword Dictionary for Restaurant and Hotel Reviews   In order to derive suitable keyword dictionaries for the target domain, we leverage a manually annotated corpus of English and German hospitality reviews in which 6,490 text spans have been categorised with a thematic aspect. For example, the span 'the waiter was very attentive' is categorised as *Service*. We aggregate all text spans for each category and filter for content words (i.e., nouns and adjectives) that are (a) common for the particular category and (b) uncommon for the other categories. Lastly, we manually filter out words for which there is no clear semantic relationship with the category *per se*.

Table 3 shows the different thematic aspects and the number of text spans associated with each. As can be seen, there is a large skew in the distribution over the categories such that the number of spans available ranges from 234 to 1,458 (German) and from 221 to 1,179 (English), which is also reflected in the resulting keyword dictionaries, whose sizes range from 28 to 120 and 18 to 173, respectively. This is, on the one hand, rooted in the distribution of the dataset, i.e., the number of text spans per category results from the overall frequencies in a small subset of reviews. On the other hand, the variety in the descriptions of the attributes per category is also different. We find a much richer vocabulary for descriptions of food, its preparation, and quality in comparison to content that refers to the pricing (cf. Table 4). This is in line with the distributions we found in the resources that were created by Di Sorbo et al. (2016) and adapted by Gao et al. (2019). Additionally, we keep the size of the dictionaries

Category	Text Spans		Keywords	
	de	en	de	en
Ambiance	519	320	33	34
Facilities	234	221	28	81
Food	1,458	1,179	120	173
Service	1,085	763	98	36
Value	374	337	91	18
Total	3,670	2,820	370	324

Table 3: Overview of annotated text spans for each category in restaurant reviews, and the number of derived keywords for each dictionary.

Category	Keywords
Food	fondue, rosti, spaghetti, risotto, clams, pizzas ..., cappuccino, cocktail, wine, whisky, ..., coffees, pastries, sauce, ..., meat, fish, ..., taste, flavour, ..., veggie, vegan, gluten, ..., breakfast, brunch, lunch, dinner, ..., starters, appetiser, entrées, desserts, ... offers, option, combination, specialties, ... plate, courses, dishes, ..., allergies, ingredients, ...
Value	affordability, money, prices, price, charge, budget, value, fortune, cost, penny, pricing, price/quality, costs, fee, expense, price-performance, competitiveprices

Table 4: Example for keyword lists for the two categories *Food* and *Value*

approximately in the same range. Although it would be possible to expand these keyword lists further with corpus-based methods, we opt to compile them in such a way that the approach is comparable to previous work.

3.3 Evaluation and Results

We evaluate the performance of the proposed approach using automatic metrics which typically compare a system output hypothesis to its corresponding ground-truth reference. We report results using the following metrics:

BLEU (Papineni et al., 2001), a precision-based metric popular in machine translation evaluation, is commonly used for evaluating performance of response and dialogue generation systems (e.g., Zhao et al. (2019), Gao et al. (2019), Ghazvininejad et al. (2018), Xu et al. (2017), Li et al. (2016), Sordoni et al. (2015), among others) since it is claimed to correlate well with human judgements. BLEU-N calculates the number of N-gram matches between a hypothesis and one or more references and is commonly reported as the weighted average score for values of N ranging from $[1, 4]$.

ROUGE (Lin, 2004) is, in contrast to BLEU, a recall-oriented metric and is often applied in the evaluation of text summarisation systems. There are two main variants of ROUGE, namely ROUGE-N and ROUGE-L. The first of these considers the number of N-grams in a reference that are matched in the corresponding hypothesis. Typical values for N are 1 and 2. ROUGE-L, on the other hand, does not presuppose a defined sequence length, but simply computes the longest common sub-sequence between a set of references and a hypothesis text.[6]

Distinct-N was proposed by Li et al. (2016) in order to measure textual diversity in neural dialogue system output. Calculated over the whole test corpus, it measures the ratio of unique N-grams to

---

[6]We use the implementation provided at `https://pypi.org/project/rouge-score/` (last accessed: July 16, 2020).

Dataset	Model	BLEU	RGE-1	RGE-2	RGE-L	DIST-1	DIST-2	BERT-F1
Hosp. (en)	s2s (baseline)	**8.17**	**35.62**	**14.55**	**28.94**	0.00	0.01	**4.82**
	s2s +A +K	2.92	24.24	9.65	20.34	0.00	0.01	-13.07
Hosp. (de)	s2s (baseline)	**10.19**	**34.26**	**15.07**	27.14	0.07	0.13	**16.81**
	s2s +A +K	8.22	32.98	14.99	**27.39**	**0.15**	**0.27**	14.86
Apps (orig.)	s2s (baseline)	14.22	32.20	13.05	24.16	0.06	0.28	-4.76
	s2s +A +K	**29.36**	**44.33**	**27.29**	**37.69**	**0.09**	**0.62**	**14.18**
Apps (uniq.)	s2s (baseline)	15.22	33.82	13.33	25.74	0.05	0.27	-0.36
	s2s +A +K	**24.84**	**40.34**	**22.59**	**33.90**	**0.06**	**0.37**	**7.17**

Table 5: Results of automatic evaluations for hospitality (hosp.) review response generation. 's2s' stands for the basic attentional seq2seq model with no additional attributes, while 's2s +A +K' stands for the seq2seq model extended with additional attribute and keyword components, as proposed by Gao et al. (2019).

the total number of N-grams generated, thus providing an indication of how varied the generated responses are.

BERTScore was recently proposed by Zhang et al. (2020) for natural language generation evaluation. It utilises contextualised word embeddings from a pre-trained BERT language model (Devlin et al., 2019)[7] and calculates the pairwise cosine similarity score between tokens in a hypothesis and tokens in a set of references. Furthermore, BERTScore incorporates importance weighting by applying the inverse document frequency (idf) score to each reference word, which is calculated on the test corpus references. The major advantage of this metric is that it alleviates the constraint of surface-form and structural similarity imposed by N-gram matching metrics, and in addition, it is applicable in multiple settings since it relies solely on a task-agnostic pre-trained BERT model.

Table 5 shows the results of our experiments in which we apply the extended seq2seq model proposed by Gao et al. (2019) to the domain of hospitality reviews in both English and German. Since we aim to inspect potential performance improvements gained by incorporating the additional feature attributes described in Section 2.3, we use the basic attentional seq2seq model as our baseline. As can be seen, the extended architecture fails to outperform the baseline according to almost all metrics in the hospitality domain. The starkest difference occurs with English, where the baseline outperforms the extended approach by considerable margins across the board. The story is slightly different in the case of German, where the margins are much smaller, but still, the superiority of the baseline seq2seq model is apparent.

The low scores for both Distinct-N metrics, particularly for English hospitality responses suggest extensive N-gram repetition. Manual inspection of the system outputs confirms that the current seq2seq models tend to generate overly generic and uninformative responses such as in Example 1, as well as showing other signs of text *degeneration* (Holtzman et al., 2020). For this reason, we avoid conducting human evaluation on these outputs and aim to address this issue in future work.

As a point of reference, we also reproduce the experiment by Gao et al. (2019) on their original app review-response dataset and on a deduplicated version which removes overlap between train and test splits (shown as 'uniq.' in Table 5)[8]. Here, we see a convincing boost in performance over the vanilla seq2seq model (15.14 BLEU points), demonstrating that the additional features do indeed help for app review response generation.

---

[7]For English, BERTScore uses a 24-layer RoBERTa Large model, while for German, a 12-layer multilingual BERT model is used to compute the contextualised embedding representations.

[8]Note, the deduplicated app dataset ensures that there is no information leakage between training, test and validation splits. As expected, there is a slight drop in performance for all metrics. However, the benefits of the extended seq2seq archticure are still clearly visible over the baseline.

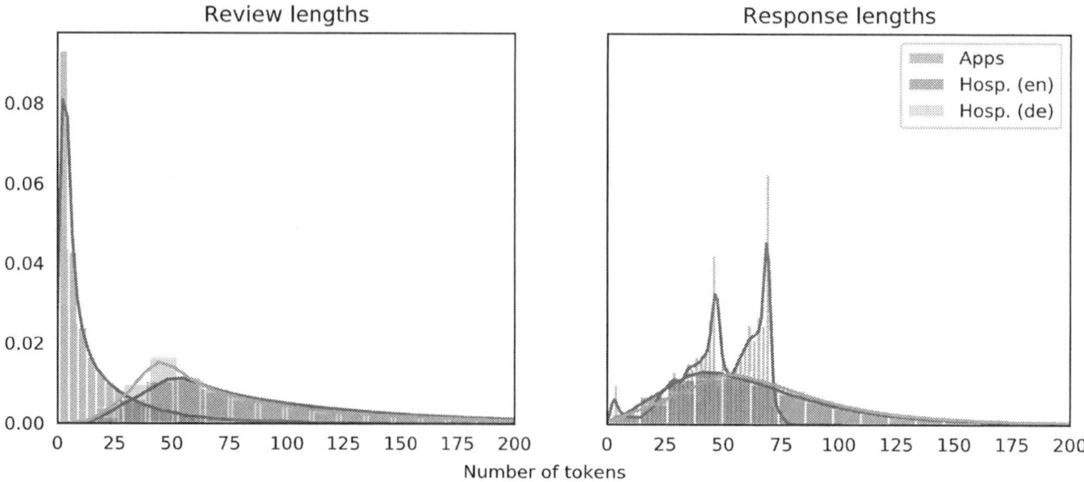

Figure 1: Distribution of review and response text lengths in the app dataset compared to the English and German hospitality datasets.

The large drop in performance of 20+ BLEU points when applying the proposed approach to a different domain and also another language is conspicuous. Therefore, in the following section, we discuss the nature of the different datasets and conduct an empirical investigation to determine potential causes.

3.4   Discussion

Given the results presented in Table 5, it is clear that the extended seq2seq architecture has difficulty generating suitable review responses when applied to the target domain. In order to investigate why this is the case, we take a closer look at the two different types of datasets and identify two potential causes, namely review length and textual variance in the responses.

Review Length   The first noticeable difference between the review-response data for apps and that for the hospitality domain is the length of the source and target texts. Figure 1 shows the distribution of text lengths for all the three datasets. As can be seen, reviews for apps (blue on left) are generally much shorter in length than reviews for hotels and restaurants, with an average length of 16 tokens for the former and approximately 100 tokens for the latter. Furthermore, the distribution of app review response lengths (blue on right) is also far from a normal distribution, with multiple peaks corresponding to response text lengths of approximately 3, 45 and 70 tokens. This is largely due to a high number of frequently occurring template responses (e.g., 'thank you !').

In theory, an attentional encoder-decoder network should be able to comfortably handle source texts of 200 tokens in length. However, we conjecture that the brevity of app reviews contributes to the simplicity of generating these responses as the input signal is far less complex in many cases.

Textual Variance in Responses   The non-normal distribution of app review response lengths raises considerable suspicion into the composition of the original app dataset. Inspecting the textual variance, i.e., the ratio of unique texts to the total number of texts, reveals that a large portion of reviews, responses and even review-response pairs occur multiple times in the app dataset. Table 6 shows textual variance among the three datasets.

As can be seen, only 40% of the responses in the app dataset are unique in contrast to approximately 94% for both English and German hospitality responses. This finding clearly indicates extensive repetition in the app dataset due to the frequent use of templated responses by app developers, which has also been reported by Hassan et al. (2018). For restaurant and hotel reviews, the story is closer to what we would expect, showing that the vast majority of responses are indeed unique. Naturally, this makes the

	Hosp. (en)	Hosp. (de)	Apps
Reviews	100.0%	99.99%	**70.04%**
Responses	94.2%	94.5%	**40.07%**
Review-response pairs	100.0%	100.0%	**88.09%**

Table 6: Percentage of unique review, response and review-response pair texts in each dataset.

task of learning to generate suitable responses in the hospitality domain much more challenging.

4   Conclusion and Future Work

We have applied a system designed for app review response generation to the domain of hospitality reviews in both English and German. According to a range of automatic evaluation metrics, the results of our experiments indicate that the benefits provided by the extended seq2seq model proposed by Gao et al. (2019) for their application domain do not transfer to our target domain. A subsequent empirical investigation into the different datasets has revealed that the nature of review-response pairs in the domain of smartphone app reviews differs significantly to that of the hospitality domain.

Given our results, we have established a preliminary baseline for automated review response generation in the domain of English and German hospitality reviews that uses a classic attentional seq2seq architecture. In future work, we intend to continue investigating potential improvements for this task, incorporating improved aspect-level sentiment detection and knowledge grounding techniques, as well as conducting more detailed evaluations with the help of human judges.

Acknowledgements

We are grateful to our industry partner re:spondelligent and the Swiss Innovation Agency InnoSuisse for their support of the ReAdvisor project (project number 38943.1 IP-ICT).

References

John Arevalo, Thamar Solorio, Manuel Montes-y-Gómez, and Fabio A. González. 2017. Gated Multimodal Units for Information Fusion. *arXiv:1702.01992 [cs, stat]*, February.

Dzmitry Bahdanau, Kyunghyun Cho, and Yoshua Bengio. 2015. Neural machine translation by jointly learning to align and translate. In Yoshua Bengio and Yann LeCun, editors, *Proceedings of the 3rd International Conference on Learning Representations (ICLR)*, San Diego, CA, USA.

Jacob Devlin, Ming-Wei Chang, Kenton Lee, and Kristina Toutanova. 2019. BERT: Pre-training of Deep Bidirectional Transformers for Language Understanding. *arXiv:1810.04805 [cs]*, May.

Andrea Di Sorbo, Sebastiano Panichella, Carol V. Alexandru, Junji Shimagaki, Corrado A. Visaggio, Gerardo Canfora, and Harald C. Gall. 2016. What would users change in my app? summarizing app reviews for recommending software changes. In *Proceedings of the 2016 24th ACM SIGSOFT International Symposium on Foundations of Software Engineering - FSE 2016*, pages 499–510, Seattle, WA, USA. ACM Press.

Cuiyun Gao, Jichuan Zeng, Xin Xia, David Lo, Michael R. Lyu, and Irwin King. 2019. Automating App Review Response Generation. In *2019 34th IEEE/ACM International Conference on Automated Software Engineering (ASE)*, pages 163–175, San Diego, USA, November. IEEE.

Marjan Ghazvininejad, Chris Brockett, Ming-Wei Chang, Bill Dolan, Jianfeng Gao, Wen-tau Yih, and Michel Galley. 2018. A knowledge-grounded neural conversation model. In *Proceedings of the Thirty-Second AAAI Conference on Artificial Intelligence*, pages 5110–5117, New Orleans, USA.

Edouard Grave, Piotr Bojanowski, Prakhar Gupta, Armand Joulin, and Tomas Mikolov. 2018. Learning Word Vectors for 157 Languages. *arXiv:1802.06893 [cs]*, March.

Safwat Hassan, Chakkrit Tantithamthavorn, Cor-Paul Bezemer, and Ahmed E. Hassan. 2018. Studying the dialogue between users and developers of free apps in the Google Play Store. *Empirical Software Engineering*, 23(3):1275–1312, June.

Ari Holtzman, Jan Buys, Li Du, Maxwell Forbes, and Yejin Choi. 2020. The Curious Case of Neural Text Degeneration. *arXiv:1904.09751 [cs]*, February.

C. Hutto and Eric Gilbert. 2014. VADER: A parsimonious rule-based model for sentiment analysis of social media text. In *Proceedings of the 12th International AAAI Conference on Web and Social Media*, Ann Arbor, Michigan, USA,.

Diederik P. Kingma and Jimmy Ba. 2017. Adam: A Method for Stochastic Optimization. *arXiv:1412.6980 [cs]*, January.

Jiwei Li, Michel Galley, Chris Brockett, Jianfeng Gao, and Bill Dolan. 2016. A Diversity-Promoting Objective Function for Neural Conversation Models. *arXiv:1510.03055 [cs]*, June.

Chunyu Li, Geng Cui, and Ling Peng. 2017. The signaling effect of management response in engaging customers: A study of the hotel industry. *Tourism Management*, 62:42–53, October.

Chunyu Li, Geng Cui, and Ling Peng. 2018. Tailoring management response to negative reviews: The effectiveness of accommodative versus defensive responses. *Computers in Human Behavior*, 84:272–284, July.

Chin-Yew Lin. 2004. ROUGE: A Package for Automatic Evaluation of Summaries. In *Text Summarization Branches Out: Proceedings of the ACL-04 Workshop*.

Stephen W. Litvin, Ronald E. Goldsmith, and Bing Pan. 2008. Electronic word-of-mouth in hospitality and tourism management. *Tourism Management*, 29(3):458–468, June.

Minh-Thang Luong, Hieu Pham, and Christopher D. Manning. 2015. Effective Approaches to Attention-based Neural Machine Translation. *arXiv:1508.04025 [cs]*, September.

Kishore Papineni, Salim Roukos, Todd Ward, and Wei-Jing Zhu. 2001. BLEU: A method for automatic evaluation of machine translation. In *Proceedings of the 40th Annual Meeting on Association for Computational Linguistics - ACL '02*, page 311, Philadelphia, Pennsylvania. Association for Computational Linguistics.

Jeffrey Pennington, Richard Socher, and Christopher Manning. 2014. Glove: Global Vectors for Word Representation. In *Proceedings of the 2014 Conference on Empirical Methods in Natural Language Processing (EMNLP)*, pages 1532–1543, Doha, Qatar. Association for Computational Linguistics.

Robert Remus, Uwe Quasthoff, and Gerhard Heyer. 2010. SentiWS – a Publicly Available German-language Resource for Sentiment Analysis. *Proceedings of the 7th International Language Ressources and Evaluation (LREC)*, pages 1168–1171.

Alexander M. Rush, Sumit Chopra, and Jason Weston. 2015. A Neural Attention Model for Abstractive Sentence Summarization. *arXiv:1509.00685 [cs]*, September.

Alessandro Sordoni, Michel Galley, Michael Auli, Chris Brockett, Yangfeng Ji, Margaret Mitchell, Jian-Yun Nie, Jianfeng Gao, and Bill Dolan. 2015. A Neural Network Approach to Context-Sensitive Generation of Conversational Responses. *arXiv:1506.06714 [cs]*, June.

Ilya Sutskever, Oriol Vinyals, and Quoc V. Le. 2014. Sequence to Sequence Learning with Neural Networks. *arXiv:1409.3215 [cs]*, December.

Mike Thelwall, Kevan Buckley, Georgios Paltoglou, Di Cai, and Arvid Kappas. 2010. Sentiment strength detection in short informal text. *Journal of the American Society for Information Science and Technology*, 61(12):2544–2558, December.

Karsten Michael Tymann, Matthias Lutz, Patrick Palsbröker, and Carsten Gips. 2019. GerVADER - A German adaptation of the VADER sentiment analysis tool for social media texts. In *Proceedings of the Conference on "Lernen, Wissen, Daten, Analysen" (LWDA)*, pages 178–189, Berlin, Germany.

Oriol Vinyals and Quoc Le. 2015. A Neural Conversational Model. *arXiv:1506.05869 [cs]*, July.

Anbang Xu, Zhe Liu, Yufan Guo, Vibha Sinha, and Rama Akkiraju. 2017. A New Chatbot for Customer Service on Social Media. In *Proceedings of the 2017 CHI Conference on Human Factors in Computing Systems*, pages 3506–3510, Denver, USA, May. ACM.

Tianyi Zhang, Varsha Kishore, Felix Wu, Kilian Q. Weinberger, and Yoav Artzi. 2020. BERTScore: Evaluating Text Generation with BERT. *arXiv:1904.09675 [cs]*, February.

Lujun Zhao, Kaisong Song, Changlong Sun, Qi Zhang, Xuanjing Huang, and Xiaozhong Liu. 2019. Review Response Generation in E-Commerce Platforms with External Product Information. In *The World Wide Web Conference on - WWW '19*, pages 2425–2435, San Francisco, CA, USA. ACM Press.

On a Chatbot Navigating a User through a Concept-Based Knowledge Model

Elizaveta Goncharova
National Research University
Higher School of Economics
Moscow, Russia
egoncharova@hse.ru

Dmitry Ilvovsky
National Research University
Higher School of Economics
Moscow, Russia
dilvovsky@hse.ru

Boris Galitsky
Oracle Inc.
Redwood Shores, CA, USA
boris.galitsky@
oracle.com

Abstract

Information retrieval chatbots are widely used as assistants, to help users formulate their requirements about the products they want to purchase, and navigate to the set of items that satisfies their requirements in the best way. The work of the modern chatbots is based mostly on the deep learning theory behind the knowledge model that can improve the performance of the system. In our work, we are developing a concept-based knowledge model that encapsulates objects and their common descriptions. The leveraging of the concept-based knowledge model allows the system to refine the initial users' requests and lead them to the set of objects with the maximal variability of parameters that matters less to them. Introducing the additional textual characteristics allows users to formulate their initial query as a phrase in natural language, rather than as some standard request in the form of, "Attribute - value".

1 Introduction

In recent years, a number of chatbots for products and services exploration has been proposed (Ukpabi and Karjaluoto, 2019; Gao et al., 2019).

Chatbots are noticeably one of the most popular AI technologies across the world. From simplifying business workflows, enhancing employee and customer experience to reducing costs, chatbots provide numerous benefits for organizations of all sizes. Besides Customer Service, chatbots support sales, marketing, IT Helpdesk, business intelligence, Intranet, and HR. The use cases of chatbots are diverse and vary across departments and industries. Most enterprise leaders are yet to understand and explore the full potential of chatbots. In spite of the efforts spent on scientific philosophy of chatbots, most are yet to produce systems capable of an efficient deployment in real-world environments. These efforts are mostly spent on a learning theory behind the conception of the chatbots. Today's level of scientific knowledge is way ahead of the real-world deployment of chatbots.

Dialogue management is one of the bottlenecks of a successful chatbot, and regretfully each of the above domains requires a specialized dialogue structure. Some dialogue structures are covered by discourse representations of the text being communicated. An exploration of products with features and attributes requires a distinct navigational structure such as lattice (a partially ordered set of pairs of product lists and features they share). In (Makhalova et al., 2019) the authors have explored how a user can walk along a lattice picking a product he needs. Once products and their features are available, we build a lattice and navigate it. However, features of products are not always available in explicit way of direct association, in a form of a database: frequently, they need to be extracted from text.

In this paper, we extract associations between products and features from text. To do that, we first reveal product names as entities, together with their features and attributes, from a corpus of documents. Then the noun phrases for products are aggregated, grouped, filtered, and cleaned. Also, these noun phrases need to occur in opinionated expressions. Moreover, we conduct an argumentation analysis giving a preference to product features being the subject of argumentative expressions of the users in their reviews.

Proceedings of the Workshop on Natural Language Processing in E-Commerce (EComNLP), pages 53–65
Barcelona, Spain (Online), Dec 12, 2020.

Opinion mining or sentiment analysis detects customers' opinions, sentiments, emotions, appraisals, and attitudes towards products and services. Chatbots employ NLP and sentiment analysis for multiple purposes including human-machine communication applied to business, education, and health.

The paper is organized as follows. In Section 2 we present the basic description of the proposed model. In Section 3 we overview the algorithm for textual data preparation. In Section 4 we give a brief overview of the proposed knowledge-based model. In the 5th section we describe the possible scenarios for navigation through the model. In section 6 we provide a few examples of the dialogue conducted by the proposed chatbot model. We conclude and give the directions for future work in Section 7.

2 Model description

Information retrieval (IR) chatbots represent systems that provide web search in case of imprecise queries in specific domains. In many cases the user has only general idea about the product he wants to purchase, so, the goal of IR chatbots is to help the user to find the desired item, and simultaneously to refine his initial idea about the product.

While the work of the standard IR chatbots is based on sending simple queries to the database and requiring the user to refine the set of predefined standard, or catalog, features (the price, e.g.), knowledge-based IR models have proved their effectiveness w.r.t. to the ability to interactively refine the query. For example, (Makhalova et al., 2019) proposed lattice navigation chatbot model that incorporates a concept-based knowledge model and an index-guided traversal through it to ensure the discovery of information relevant for users and coherent to their preferences. This chatbot not only supports a search session, but also helps users to discover properties of items and sequentially refine an imprecise query. However, it enables the chatbot to process only the standard features, and ignores text descriptions of an object, which could allow the users to grasp some additional characteristics of the product he wants to buy. In our work we propose to enlarge the proposed in (Makhalova et al., 2019) knowledge model with the additional characteristics, extracted from textual descriptions of the products.

The online stores usually contain a database of digital reviews, where a person may refer to find some additional information about the product. If we encapsulate this kind of information into the knowledge model, the system will be able to provide more additional characteristics to the user, while the user can formulate his requests not just in the "attribute - value" form, but also as the phrase in natural language.

The pipeline shown in Figure 1 illustrates the scheme of the proposed IR system. It combines several blocks of data preparation responsible for retrieving the informative features from the text and enlarging the catalog data, building the lattice-based knowledge model, and navigation through the lattice with the chatbot to retrieve the information relevant for the user.

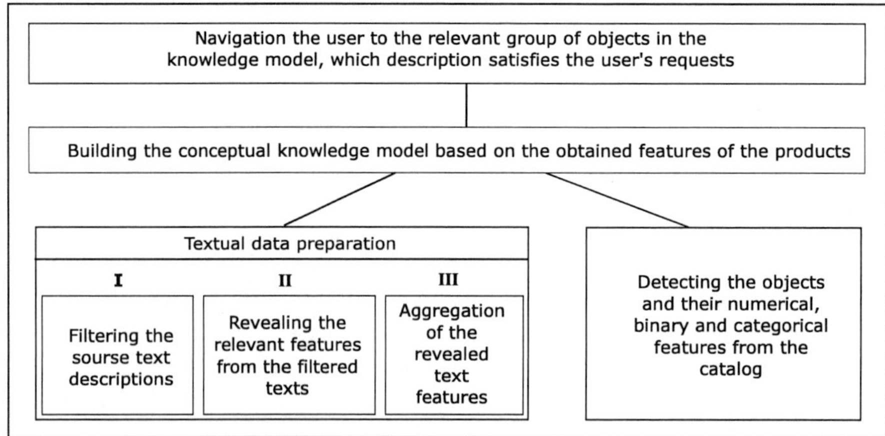

Figure 1: The proposed pipeline includes three main blocks: preparation of the text data, building the knowledge model, and navigation through the model

3   Textual data preparation

Let us overview the pipeline that illustrates the main blocks of the proposed IR system. The first block is the preparation of textual data that we have divided into three parts. The first part is responsible for filtering the initial text descriptions, which is especially important when the source of information is the users' feedbacks. We would like to retrieve text features only from the useful, or reasoned reviews, hence, we need to filter the initial texts by their validity. In the second step, the system reveals informative parts from the filtered text descriptions. On the one hand, this part of the pipeline allows the system to reduce the size of processed data and, on the other hand, to process only those parts of texts that refer to the object characteristics. We perform this part via parsing the initial paragraph of the text and retrieving the noun phrases as the most common descriptors of the object. The final step is responsible for aggregation of the text features. Some noun phrases occur only in several reviews, which means that this description of an object is not supported by many users, so we claim that it is a plain biased opinion, and the system does not use these descriptors. We propose to use only the features that are revealed from 30% percent of the reviews. In the following subsections, we will describe each part of the first block in more detail.

3.1   Filtering text data

At this stage, the system identifies useful reviews in the initial dataset. We assume that useful reviews that we should consider during the follow-up procedure of text features retrieval should include some argumentation part rather than just sentiment or plain opinion about the product. If we filter out the useless reviews, the system will gather informative text features only from the feedbacks that contain some reasons or evidence of why the product is good or bad. Argument mining techniques are able to capture these specificity of the text. So, we propose to classify the reviews w.r.t. to their argumentative power.

Argument mining itself is a challenging NLP task, nowadays the researchers find different ways to solve it. In our project, we investigate the influence of various features on the results of argumentation mining. We build a binary classifier that divides the feedbacks into the argumentative and non-argumentative ones. The classifier is based on simple linguistic features, such as tf-idf or bag of words, and some additional features corresponding to the argumentation, which are believed to improve the classification performance.

The one source of argumentation features that we utilize in our discriminative model is the automatic MARGOT tool, which is an online argumentation mining system. The MARGOT provides the segmentation of the text on claim and premise parts and reveals several scores that outline the power of claim and evidence in the sentence. Another additional source of information is discourse. There are research (Musi et al., 2018; Hewett et al., 2019) that prove the strong correlation between the rhetoric relation and argumentation relations in the texts. We use state-of-the-art discourse parser that can detect the discourse connections among the text parts, and argue that if we enlarge the linguistic features of the text described above with some discourse information, we can also improve the performance of our classifier. In further subsections we briefly describe these two additional argumentation characteristics.

3.1.1   Argumentation filtering

We use MARGOT system as a source of additional features that could improve the performance of detection argumentative reviews. MARGOT is publicly available argumentation mining system that performs two tasks, the former is segmentation of text into claim and premise, and the latter is the detection of claim and evidence scores for each sentence in the input text. These scores are used to assess the strength of claim and evidence. We propose to encapsulate these scores as the additional characteristics that will be used by our classifier for argument presence detection.

In (Passon et al., 2018), the authors propose to calculate the statistics of how many sentences in the review were defined by MARGOT as argumentative and use this statistics as the additional features. In our research we do not calculate such kind of information, however, we compute two additional characteristics for the claim and evidence scores, respectively. These features are calculated as the maximum claim score detected for each sentence, and the maximum evidence score, which is also detected for each sentence in the text. These characteristics simply define if the text contains at least one argument component or not: $score_{cl} = max_{s \in S}(score_{claim})$, $score_{ev} = max_{s \in S}(score_{evidence})$, where S is a set of sentences compiling the review, $score_{evidence}$ ($score_{claim}$) is the evidence (claim) score calculated by the MARGOT system for these sentences of the review. So, this additional information enlarges our data and improves the performance of the argument classifier.

The examples below show the output of the MARGOT system for two reviews and the $score_{cl}$ and $score_{ev}$ calculated for these reviews.

R_1: In my opinion, the 2020 MacBook Air is a perfect laptop. It has physical keys that are a pleasure to type on, a beautiful screen, an optimal size, good pricing, and a quad-core processor.

R_2: Simply, DON'T buy it!

	MARGOT output		Calculated features	
Text	$score_{evidence}$	$score_{claim}$	$score_{ev}$	$score_{cl}$
In my opinion , the 2020 MacBook Air is a perfect laptop.	0.11	-0.96		
It has physical keys that are a pleasure to type on, a beautiful screen, an optimal size, good pricing, and a quad-core processor.	-0.12	-0.27	0.11	-0.27
Simply, DON'T buy it!	No argument components have been found		None	None

So, the first review was defined by the MARGOT as argumentative, as its maximum evidence score is above zero. Clearly, this is a useful review. The reviewer expresses his opinion about a product and specifies its parameters that have motivated his satisfaction with the product. While the author of the second review expressed just his plain opinion about the product and did not explain it in any way. There the MARGOT system outputs that there is no argumentation in the text, and we omit this text from further processing.

3.1.2 Discourse features

As another source of additional information that could be useful in detecting the argumented review, we utilize the discourse features. During recent years the researchers have revealed a strong correlation between argumentation and discourse relations (Mann and Thompson, 1988) that could be retrieved from the rhetoric structure of the text. The investigation in this sphere claims that the discourse features can represent the corresponding argument relation (Galitsky et al., 2018). For example, the argumentation relation detail corresponds to elaboration relation in RST, while antithesis in rhetoric structure theory (RST) could correspond to the attack argument. Thus, when the one deals with the task of argument mining it seems reasonable to use information obtained from the RST, and utilize the discourse features in order to find some argument structure or simply detect the existence of argumentative relation in the text. Several effective discourse parsers could be used for making the automatic rhetoric parsing of the input text (Ji and Eisenstein, 2014; Lin and Kan, 2014).

We derive features such as elaboration, purpose, antithesis, circumstance, etc. from the discourse tree obtained with (Ji and Eisenstein, 2014) parser. We treat them as categorical features and encode using one-hot encoding. Further, these characteristics enlarge the input data and train an XGBoost classifier (Chen and Guestrin, 2016) to predict whether an argument relation exists.

The training data used for our research is obtained from the public Amazon Reviews dataset (McAuley and Leskovec, 2013). This dataset contains the users' evaluation of some product, text of the review, and metadata. Metadata contains the rating of the review (whether it was judged by other users as useful, or not). We split all the reviews into two classes in accordance with their rating of usefulness. If at least 70% of the people who voted the review judged it as useful, the review goes to the positive class, in another case — to the negative. Then we train the classifier to detect the useful and not useful reviews.

3.2 Revealing relevant textual features

After the system cleaned the data by filtering out useless reviews it proceeds to retrieve relevant features from these filtered texts. By relevant features, we mean the parts of the text which correspond to the description of a product. For example, in the sentence *"I think this is a good laptop"* only the phrase *"good laptop"* is referred to as an object description, while other words are irrelevant for our task and should be omitted.

We believe that noun phrases are the main descriptors of an object. For example, *[NP (a beautiful screen), [NP (good laptop)].* To identify such object descriptors we parse the sentences of the reviews and construct the parse trees, then we reveal only noun phrases and keep them as the description of some specific product.

This procedure refers to the second stage of data preparation. Obtained features are believed to express some characteristics of the product, however, if the descriptors were revealed from one or two reviews out of hundreds, it is rather a biased opinion of some particular reviewer, than the objective one. So as the final stage of data preparation we propose to aggregate the reviews into the groups and use only those descriptors that are supported by some predefined percentage of the reviewers.

3.3 Data aggregation

Data aggregation allows the system to combine noun phrases into groups and use the phrase as a feature to describe an object, only if it has occurred in some percentage of useful reviews. To provide this we calculate pairs consisting of the reviews and their common descriptions in the form of the noun phrases (Strok et al., 2014). These pairs are called concepts, and the order defined for them makes an algebraic lattice, called concept lattice (Galitsky et al., 2013).

3.3.1 Knowledge-based model

To construct the lattice and aggregate the descriptors (the noun phrases) we apply pattern structures (Ganter and Kuznetsov, 2001) that is defined as a triple $(G, (D, \sqcap), \delta)$, where G is a set of objects, $(D, \sqcap)$ is a complete meet-semilattice of descriptions and $\delta \rightarrow D$ is mapping an object to a description. The Galois connection between set of objects and their descriptions is also defined as follows $A^\square = \sqcap_{g \in A} \delta(g)$, $d^\square = \{g \in G | d \sqsubseteq \delta(g)\}$ for $A \subseteq G$, for $d \in D$.

A pair $< A, d >$ for which $A^\square = d$ and $d^\square = A$ is called a pattern concept. So, if we treat A as the set of texts describing each product and d as their common description, we can calculate the concept lattice. At each level of the lattice, the concepts provide different degrees of data aggregation. Starting from the most specific concepts $< A_1, d_1 >$ at the first level of the lattice, where A_1 consists of just one review, and d_1 is the set of all possible noun phrases constituting the review from A_1, and ending with the final concept $< A_{last}, d_{last} >$, where A_{last} is the set of all reviews about some particular product, and d_{last} is a set of noun phrases that are common for all the reviews.

To calculate the concepts we imply the following steps:

- Consider the set of texts (users reviews on some specific product) R.

- For each review $r_i \in R$ calculate the set of their noun phrases $\delta(r_i)$.

- Build pattern structure for the reviews R and their descriptions applying standard algorithm (AddIntent (van der Merwe et al., 2004) or CbO (Kuznetsov, 1993)). The intersection operation $\sqcap$ for descriptions is defined as follows, parts of speech tags are strictly match, while the word vertices themselves are labeled by wildcards (*).

Let us consider a small example of four users' reviews about some laptop from the Amazon web site and build a lattice with the algorithm proposed above.

R_1: In my opinion, the 2020 MacBook Air is a perfect laptop. It has physical keys that are a pleasure to type on, a beautiful screen, an optimal size, good pricing, and a quad-core processor.

R_2: The MacBook Air is an extremely slow laptop. Right out the box it was slow and even after updating it is still slow and seems to only be getting slower day by day.

R_3: *The new magic keys are amazing when typing. Unlike the 2019 MacBook Air. It's so amazing how you pay $999 for double the storage you got form last year that's starts at $1099. It is very fast and smooth.*

R_4: *The 2020 MacBook Air is a perfect laptop due to its good pricing.*

In Figure 2 there is a diagram of pattern structure lattice constructed for these reviews.

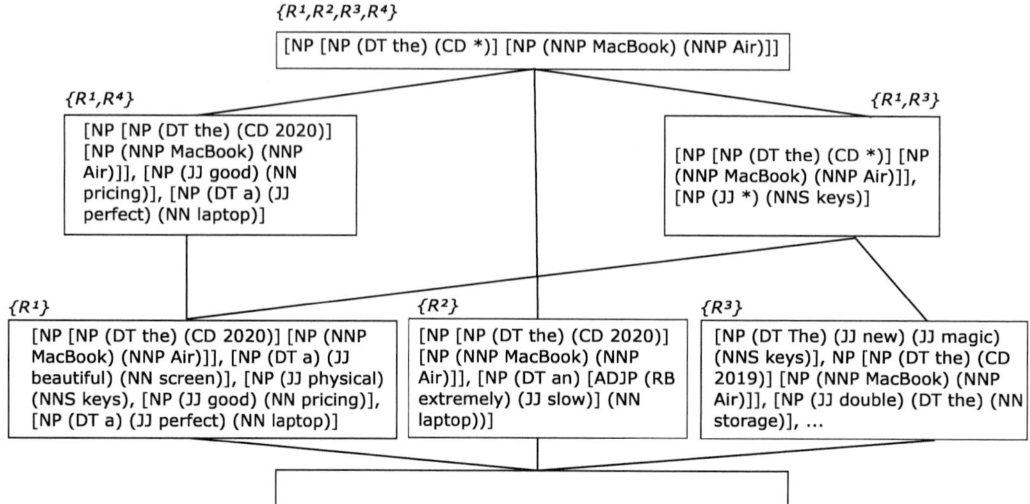

Figure 2: Diagram of the pattern structure lattice for the reviews

At the first level of the lattice diagram, we get concepts that correspond to the reviews themselves. In our running example we can see that the reviews are about some specific laptop and its characteristics: [NP [NP (DT the) (CD 2020)] [NP (NNP MacBook) (NNP Air)]], [NP (DT a) (JJ beautiful) (NN screen)], [NP (JJ physical) (NNS keys)]. At the next level, we observe a pairwise intersection of the reviews. There, the description of the review R_4 includes the description of the review R_1 ($\delta(R_4)$ is more general than ($\delta(R_1)$), and the description of the review R_2 is not supported by any other review. The top-level concept contains phrases, which are common for all texts. In this case, the most common phrase characterizes the brand of the laptop.

As we can see the initial noun phrases revealed for the product (the union of the descriptions from the first level of the lattice) were aggregated into two more general groups. The first group consists of the common description of the reviews R_1 and R_4, and the second group is the common descriptions of R_1 and R_3. We propose to enlarge the initial data about the product with the descriptions that are supported by at least 30% of the reviewers. In our case, these are the phrases from the second and the following levels of the lattice. This aggregation of the phrases allows us to reduce the number of informative characteristics of the product by omitting the ones, which are rarely mentioned in the reviews.

We want to highlight one more detail. In the above example, the intersection operation has been defined as the strict match of the part of speech without consideration of the words themselves. However, we lose lots of important information that is decoded in the words, the sentiment or synonymy, for instance, if we have two noun phrases such as *"fast processor"* and *"quick processor"*, the intersection operation defined above provides the result of intersection as *"* processor"*. In this case, we lose the information that both the reviewers were satisfied with the speed of the processor's work.

We assume that considering the contextual word embedding provided by Bert, e.g., could improve the performance of the IR chatbot and avoid losing the important information during the text features retrieval. Thus, when we calculate the intersection between two noun phrases we should compare not just the part of speech tags, but also the embeddings of the adjectives and the nouns in order to keep the synonymy among the phrases.

4 Combination of the textual and catalog features and building the knowledge model

In the previous sections we described the preparation of text data that can be extracted from the users' reviews (or some other text descriptions of the product). Thus, we enlarge standard characteristics of the product that could be revealed from the database with its text descriptions. Based on this data we propose to build the conceptual knowledge model that will represent the data in the form of non-overlapping hierarchically organised groups of objects and their common descriptions. We have already implemented the similar approach in data aggregation block (Section 3.3.1). To build this knowledge model we also leverage pattern structures, whereas, now the set of objects is the real set of the products available in the dataset, and the description is the row in this dataset containing all the features that the system possesses about the product: the numerical, categorical, binary, and textual ones.

Based on the constructed knowledge model, the chatbot walks through the lattice and navigate the user to the group of the objects that satisfies his initial query. Simultaneously the chatbot assesses the variability of the items inside the closed concept and proposes some attributes for the refinement.

In the framework proposed in (Makhalova et al., 2019) the authors assumed that the user specifies only the numerical characteristics of the product, and the chatbot navigates the user and refines only this type of attributes, such as price, etc. Now, we can take into account both the numerical and text description of the product, and, thus, to expand the user's scope to formulate his query.

5 Navigation procedure

Once the conceptual model is built, the chatbot utilizes this information and traverses the model based on the users' requests. At the beginning of the search, the user formulates the initial query about the product he wants to purchase. This query may contain object and attribute names, values of the attributes, or object description formulated as some phrase. As a result of running the keyword query, we get the set of objects and their descriptions the user has requested, (O_q, d_q), where O_q is a set of objects satisfying this query, and d_q is the description specified by the user. From this pair, we identify the initial lattice node (O_0, d_0) whose description satisfies d_q. If the user mentioned some numerical features, the system matches the numerical values from d_q with the corresponding values in d_0. Otherwise, if the user inserted a phrase, the system retrieves its noun phrases and matches it with the textual description of the products inside a concept (O_0, d_0).

Here we present a model of the interactive search where the chatbot clarifies the user needs in the course of navigation. The chatbot looks for the concept, which satisfies the initial user's request and simultaneously keeps the variability of the attributes that the user did not refine. The specification (updating the set of constraints) for the queries continues until the user found no more appropriate specification or a product that corresponds exactly to what he searched for.

Once (O_0, d_0) is identified, we fix the lattice node and the chatbot shows the user its current position in the lattice (O_i, d_i). The chatbot calculates the diversity of the features inside the concept (Makhalova et al., 2019). If the feature is diverse then the chatbot asks the user, if he wants to refine it. Then at each iteration i the user is expected to request one of the following:

1) *update*

- specify some attributes proposed by the chatbot for refinement, thus the chatbot will reduce the set of the object of interest $O_i \rightarrow O_{i+1}$. That can be requested via the utterance *"attribute name" - "refined value"*, or *"attribute name" is more than/less than "refined value"*.
  This is a jump down the lattice as we have fewer objects and less general description.
- specify some attributes that the chatbot did not propose, however the user decided to refine it.
  This is a jump down the lattice as we have fewer objects and less general description.
- return to the previous step and to decline some of the refinements. For example, the user has refined the color of the product as *"green"*, however, he decided to look at the objects which are *"green or blue"*.
  This is a jump up the lattice as we have more objects and more general description.

2) *abrupt change of interest*

- Proceed to new set O_{i+1} . That can be requested via the utterance 'switch to O_{i+1}
- Run new query and go to (O_q, d_q) All of these three cases is a long-distance jump to a new area in the lattice.

3) *text description*

- The user may formulate its request in natural language. In this case, the system reveals the noun phrases from the parsed request and finds the correspondence among them and textual descriptions of the concepts in the knowledge model.

6 Simulation of the dialogue

In this section, we simulate the interaction of a chatbot with a user, where the knowledge model is built based on the information obtained from the small dataset presented in Table 1 (see Appendix). The textual data was prepared in accordance with the technique described in Section 3.

The knowledge model obtained for this dataset and the detailed description of some concepts is given in the Appendix.

Below we present two dialogues with the chatbot that walks through the constructed knowledge model and helps the user to purchase a tablet based on his requests.

Dialogue 1	Dialogue 2
User I am looking for a fast tablet. Apple.	**User** Tablet with the weight less than 0.5.
Bot *We have found 3 objects satisfying your requirements.*	**Bot** *We have found 4 objects satisfying you requirements.*
Tablet Apple iPad Pro 12.9 2018, Tablet Apple iPad Mini 2019, Tablet Apple iPad Air 10.5 2019	**Tablet Apple iPad Pro 12.9 2018, Tablet Apple iPad Air 10.5 2019, Tablet Apple iPad 10.2, Tablet Samsung Galaxy TAB A 8.0 2019**
Would you like to specify some of the characteristics:	Would you like to specify some of their characteristics
the price ([384.0, 960.0]),	price ([384.0, 960.0]),
weight ([0.3, 0.631]),	color ([0.3, 0.631]),
or screen size ([7.9, 12.9])?	brand ([Apple, Samsung]),
User The price should be less than 800.	screen size ([7.9, 12.9])?
Bot *We have found 2 objects satisfying you requirements.*	**User** The screen size should be more than 10, and I also want to utilize this *tablet for work.*
Tablet Apple iPad Mini 2019, Tablet Apple iPad Air 10.5 2019	**Bot** *We have found 1 object satisfying you requirements.*
Would you like to specify some of the characteristics:	**Tablet Samsung Galaxy TAB A 8.0 2019**
the battery ([5124.0; 8134.0]),	Do you want to purchase it, or start a new session?
weight ([0.3, 0.456]),	**User** Is it *a reliable tablet?*
screen size ([7.9, 10.5])?	
User No, but it should also have a bright screen.	

<table>
<tr><td>Dialogue 1</td><td>Dialogue 2</td></tr>
<tr><td>Bot Object Tablet Apple iPad Air 10.5 2019 satisfies the requirements.

Do you want to purchase it, or start a new session?

User Purchase.</td><td>Bot Unfortunately, we could not found the phrase "a reliable tablet" among the object descriptions, however, you could look at some reviews in more details.

User No.</td></tr>
</table>

As we can see, the query formulated by the user does not contain any attribute names or their values, it is a simple phrase in natural language. So, we reveal the set of noun phrases from the query (*[NP (NNP Apple)], [NP (DT a) (JJ fast) (NNP tablet)]*), and finds the corresponding concept, whose text description contains these phrases. This is the second concept, which contains three tablets (see Appendix). The system calculates the varied characteristics and proposes them to the user for refinement. In the next step, the user has chosen to specify the price. So, the chatbot walks down the lattice to the less general fifth concept and proposes new features for the refinement. The user refuses to specify the proposed features, but refines the new textual characteristics, so the chatbot moves down the lattice and finds the next less general concept, whose textual description satisfies the noun phrase *"a bright screen"*.

During the second dialogue, the user introduces the noun phrase, that is not contained in the description of any object. So, the chatbot tells the user that this phrase is not contained in the text description of the objects in the database, however, he might show the user text descriptions of the current objects, or he may want to specify another characteristic of an object. The user refuses, so, now he can start a new search session.

7 Conclusion

In the work, we have introduced a conceptual-based IR chatbot that is able to process both the standard numerical features of an object and the features retrieved from some textual descriptions.

Our work is motivated by the fact that utilizing a clear navigational structure such as lattice improves the performance of IR systems. Despite the fact that the IR systems utilizing these structures exist, none of them combines the standard numerical features with the complex features of the product that can be extracted from texts. So, in our work, we are concentrated on retrieving text features from the dataset of users' reviews, which are a great source of additional information about an item. The pipeline we introduced combines three steps of text data preparation, where we filter, extract, and aggregate the text descriptions. Thus, the final text characteristics of the object are obtained only from the argumentative texts that provide the reasons and motivation rather than plain sentiment. The features themselves are aggregated into the groups in accordance with the percentage of the reviewers that have used them to describe a product.

The introduction of the textual features to the product description enables the chatbot to process not just the standardized users queries written in the *"Attribute - value"* form, but also the requests formulated in natural language.

We also presented the simulation of the dialogue that illustrates possible scenarios of the user-chatbot interaction. While we remark that this is a preliminary study, and in the future works we will present the comparison of the proposed framework with the existing models of IR chatbots.

References

Tianqi Chen and Carlos Guestrin. 2016. Xgboost: A scalable tree boosting system. *CoRR*, abs/1603.02754.

Boris Galitsky, Dmitry Ilvovsky, Fedor Strok, and Sergei Kuznetsov. 2013. Improving text retrieval efficiency with pattern structures on parse thickets. *CEUR Workshop Proceedings*, 977:6–21, 01.

Boris A. Galitsky, Dmitry I. Ilvovsky, and Sergey O. Kuznetsov. 2018. Detecting logical argumentation in text via communicative discourse tree. *Journal of Experimental Theoretical Artificial Intelligence*, 30:637 – 663.

Bernhard Ganter and Sergei O. Kuznetsov. 2001. Pattern structures and their projections. In *Conceptual Structures: Broadening the Base*, pages 129–142, Berlin, Heidelberg. Springer Berlin Heidelberg.

Xiang Gao, Sungjin Lee, Yizhe Zhang, Chris Brockett, Michel Galley, Jianfeng Gao, and William B. Dolan. 2019. Jointly optimizing diversity and relevance in neural response generation. In *NAACL-HLT*.

Freya Hewett, Roshan Rane, Nina Harlacher, and Manfred Stede. 2019. The utility of discourse parsing features for predicting argumentation structure. pages 98–103, 01.

Yangfeng Ji and Jacob Eisenstein. 2014. Representation learning for text-level discourse parsing. volume 1, pages 13–24, 06.

Sergei Kuznetsov. 1993. A fast algorithm for computing all intersections of objects in a finite semi-lattice. *Automatic Documentation and Mathematical Linguistics*, 27:11–21, 01.

Tou Nh H. Lin, Z. and M. Kan. 2014. A pdtb-styled end-to-end discourse parser. volume 20, pages 151–184.

Tatiana P. Makhalova, Dmitry A. Ilvovsky, and Boris A. Galitsky. 2019. Information retrieval chatbots based on conceptual models. In *Graph-Based Representation and Reasoning*, pages 230–238, Cham. Springer International Publishing.

William C. Mann and Sandra A. Thompson. 1988. Rhetorical structure theory: Toward a functional theory of text organization. *Text Talk*, 8:243 – 281.

Julian J. McAuley and Jure Leskovec. 2013. Hidden factors and hidden topics: understanding rating dimensions with review text. In *RecSys '13*.

Elena Musi, Tariq Alhindi, Manfred Stede, Leonard Kriese, Smaranda Muresan, and Andrea Rocci. 2018. A multi-layer annotated corpus of argumentative text: From argument schemes to discourse relations. In *LREC*.

Marco Passon, Marco Lippi, Giuseppe Serra, and Carlo Tasso. 2018. Predicting the usefulness of amazon reviews using off-the-shelf argumentation mining. pages 35–39, 01.

Fedor Strok, Boris Galitsky, Dmitry Ilvovsky, and Sergei Kuznetsov. 2014. Pattern structure projections for learning discourse structures. In Gennady Agre, Pascal Hitzler, Adila A. Krisnadhi, and Sergei O. Kuznetsov, editors, *Artificial Intelligence: Methodology, Systems, and Applications*, pages 254–260, Cham. Springer International Publishing.

Dandison Ukpabi and Heikki Karjaluoto, 2019. *Chatbot Adoption in Tourism Services: A Conceptual Exploration*, pages 105–121. 10.

Dean van der Merwe, Sergei Obiedkov, and Derrick Kourie. 2004. Addintent: A new incremental algorithm for constructing concept lattices. In Peter Eklund, editor, *Concept Lattices*, pages 372–385, Berlin, Heidelberg. Springer Berlin Heidelberg.

Appendix

Below there is a fragment of the dataset containing the information about 6 tablets. The features of the tablets are presented as the standard numerical characteristics and their text descriptions. The graph given after the table represents the knowledge model (in the form of the concept lattice). This is a hierarchically organized set of pairs, called concepts. Each pair consists of the set of objects and their common descriptions. The concepts with the lower numbers are more general (they contain fewer objects and their description is less variable) than the ones with the higher numbers (they contain more objects and their description is more variable).

Table 1: A fragment of tablet database

	Brand	Battery	Weight	Back camera	OS	Hard memory	Size	4G LTE	Sensor	Color	Price	Text
Tablet Apple iPad Pro 12.9 2018	8	9720	0.631	12	4	4	12.90	0	1	1, 5, 6, 7, 8	960	(Apple), (fast tablet), (work) ...
Tablet Apple iPad Mini 2019	8	5124	0.3	8	4	3	7.90	0	1	1, 5, 6, 7, 8	384	(Apple), (* tablet) ...
Tablet Apple iPad Air 10.5 2019	8	8134	0.456	8	4	3	10.50	0	1	1, 5, 6, 7, 8	612	(* bright screen), (Apple), (fast tablet), (for work) ...
Tablet Dell Latitude 7200	5	5250	0.851	8	1	16	12.30	1	1	1, 8	2281	(movies and videos), ...
Tablet Apple iPad 10.2	8	8827	0.483	8	6	3	12.20	0	1	1, 5, 6, 7, 8	400	(Apple), (* tablet), , (for work) ...
Tablet Samsung Galaxy TAB A 8.0 2019	7	5100	0.345	8	5	2	8.00	0	1	1, 8	150	(for work), ...

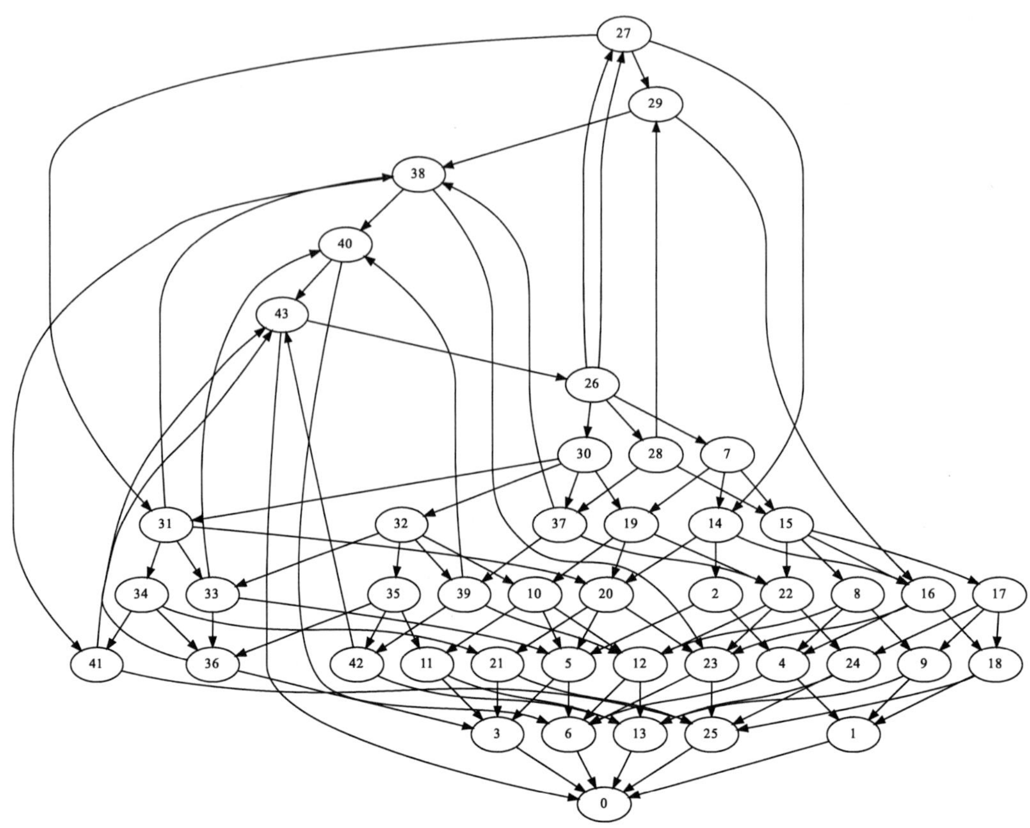

Below are the concepts that the chatbot has passed during the communication with the user in the first and second dialogues respectively.

<table>
<tr><td colspan="2" align="center">Dialogue 1</td><td colspan="2" align="center">Dialogue 1</td></tr>
<tr><td colspan="2" align="center">Concept at position 2</td><td colspan="2" align="center">Concept at position 5</td></tr>
<tr><td>Feature</td><td>Value</td><td>Feature</td><td>Value</td></tr>
<tr><td>Brand</td><td>Apple</td><td>Brand</td><td>Apple</td></tr>
<tr><td>Battery</td><td>[5124.0; 9720.0]</td><td>Battery</td><td>[5124.0; 8134.0]</td></tr>
<tr><td>Weight</td><td>[0.3; 0.631]</td><td>Weight</td><td>[0.3; 0.456]</td></tr>
<tr><td>Warranty</td><td>1</td><td>Warranty</td><td>1</td></tr>
<tr><td>Back camera</td><td>[8, 12]</td><td>Back camera</td><td>8</td></tr>
<tr><td>OS</td><td>Mac os</td><td>OS</td><td>Mac os</td></tr>
<tr><td>Hard memory</td><td>[3, 4]</td><td>Hard memory</td><td>3</td></tr>
<tr><td>Screen size</td><td>[7.9, 12.9]</td><td>Screen size</td><td>[7.9, 10.5]</td></tr>
<tr><td>4G LTE</td><td>No</td><td>4G LTE</td><td>No</td></tr>
<tr><td>Sensor</td><td>1</td><td>Sensor</td><td>1</td></tr>
<tr><td>Color</td><td>[1,5,6,7,8]</td><td>Color</td><td>[1,5,6,7,8]</td></tr>
<tr><td>Price</td><td>[384.0, 960.0]</td><td>Price</td><td>[384.0; 612.0]</td></tr>
<tr><td>Text</td><td>[NP (JJ *) (NN tablet)], [NP (JJ *) (NNS sensor)], [NP (NNP Apple)]</td><td>Text</td><td>[NP (JJ *) (NN tablet)], [NP (NNP Apple)]</td></tr>
</table>

Dialogue 2

Concept at position 31	
Feature	Value
Brand	Apple, Samsung
Battery	[5100.0; 8827.0]
Weight	[0.3; 0.483]
Warranty	1
Back camera	8
OS	Android, iOS 10, iOS last
Hard memory	[2.0; 3.0]
Screen size	[7.9; 12.2]
4G LTE	No
Sensor	1
Color	[1, 8]
Price	[150.0; 612.0]
Text	[NP (NN device)]

Dialogue 2

Concept at position 43	
Feature	Value
Brand	Samsung
Battery	[5100.0; 5100.0]
Weight	[0.345; 0.345]
Warranty	1
Back camera	8
OS	Android
Hard memory	2
Screen size	[8.0, 8.0]
4G LTE	No
Sensor	1
Color	[1,8]
Price	[150.0; 150.0]
Text	[NP (NN tablet) (NNP samsung) (NNP galaxy)], [NP (DT a) (NN laptop)) (PP (IN for) (NP (NN work))]

BERT-based similarity learning for product matching

Janusz Tracz[1], Piotr Wójcik[1], Kalina Jasinska-Kobus[1, 2],
Riccardo Belluzzo[1], Robert Mroczkowski[1], Ireneusz Gawlik[1, 3]
[1] ML Research at Allegro.pl
[2] Poznan University of Technology
[3] AGH University of Science and Technology
{janusz.tracz,piotr.wojcik,kalina.kobus,riccardo.belluzzo,
robert.mroczkowski,ireneusz.gawlik}@allegro.pl

Abstract

Product matching, i.e., being able to infer the product being sold for a merchant-created offer, is crucial for any e-commerce marketplace, enabling product-based navigation, price comparisons, product reviews, etc. This problem proves a challenging task, mostly due to the extent of product catalog, data heterogeneity, missing product representants, and varying levels of data quality. Moreover, new products are being introduced every day, making it difficult to cast the problem as a classification task.

In this work, we apply BERT-based models in a similarity learning setup to solve the product matching problem. We provide a thorough ablation study, showing the impact of architecture and training objective choices. Application of transformer-based architectures and proper sampling techniques significantly boosts performance for a range of e-commerce domains, allowing for production deployment.

1 Introduction

With more and more retailers moving their business online the number of items available on e-commerce marketplaces, such as Amazon, Alibaba or Allegro.pl, grows exponentially. In an environment with hundreds of millions of items listed for sale every day, providing a satisfactory search and purchase experience brings many challenges.

One such huge challenge for e-commerce portals is introducing product-based experience, both for the buyers and for the merchants. From the buyer's perspective, this means facilitating the search process by grouping offers that refer to the same real-world product while being sold by different merchants. Merchants, on the other hand, benefit by having access to a high-quality product catalog, which allows them to speed up the listing process and provide the buyers with more complete product descriptions. Achieving product-based experience in any e-commerce portal is only made possible by being able to automatically find offers of the same product. This process is often called product matching. Product matching in e-commerce is a non-trivial task mostly because of the large number of products, their high heterogeneity, missing product representants, and varying levels of data quality. For a more detailed overview of challenges that make product matching hard, we refer the reader to (Shah et al., 2018).

Classical approaches to product matching and its generalization (entity matching) often rely on rule-based methods and hand-crafted features such as string similarity measures (Thor, 2010; Köpcke et al., 2010; Konda et al., 2016; Brunner and Stockinger, 2019). Recent advances of deep learning in natural language processing (NLP) sparked increasing interest in end-to-end deep learning approaches both for entity matching (Brunner and Stockinger, 2020; Li et al., 2020b) and product matching (Shah et al., 2018; Ristoski et al., 2018; Li et al., 2020a). Here, we follow this trend and present our experiences with leveraging transformer-based neural language models (Vaswani et al., 2017) combined with the similarity learning setup for product matching. While transformer architectures have been very recently applied to entity matching (Brunner and Stockinger, 2020), to the best of our knowledge, we are the first

Proceedings of the Workshop on Natural Language Processing in E-Commerce (EComNLP), pages 66–75
Barcelona, Spain (Online), Dec 12, 2020.

to apply them specifically for the product matching problem in e-commerce. Aside from architectural choices, we show that sampling techniques tailored to the product matching domain prove to be crucial in the progress of similarity learning.

The contributions of our paper are as follows:

- we apply state-of-the-art BERT-based models (Devlin et al., 2019) in the similarity learning setup to solve the product matching task in the e-commerce domain,

- we compare the usefulness of modern BERT-based architectures such as BERT and DistilBERT (Sanh et al., 2019) for the product matching task,

- we propose *category hard* batch construction strategy, which proves to increase the fraction of active training triplets and the performance of the final model,

- we adopt and evaluate different batch construction strategies in the similarity learning setup for solving product matching.

This work is organized as follows. Section 2 introduces the product matching problem. Section 3 describes our approach. In Section 4 we present the experiments and results. Section 5 briefly reviews the related work on product matching. Finally, we discuss the challenges and conclude our work in Section 6.

2 Product matching

Product matching aims at identifying offers of the same product across many merchants selling it in an e-commerce portal and integrating the information into a single entry in a product catalog. An offer is an instance of a specific good described by vendor-provided information. This information may include but is not limited to, title, its text description, attributes, category, and photos. A product represents a manufacturer's description of a good and is described similarly. At a typical e-commerce marketplace, one may find many offers of the same product. Also, not all products need to have offer representatives (e.g. legacy or yet unmatched products).

Recent papers mostly focus on using only the information contained in the titles or using both titles and attributes (Li et al., 2020a). In this work, in addition to using the title and attributes information, we also make use of the category, i.e., an identifier of a set of goods of the same type.

2.1 Generalized zero-shot multi-class classification

Production use of a product matching system requires that the system is able to operate correctly for yet unrepresented products. As products are being introduced, the product matching system should be capable to handle new instances.

Motivated by this requirement, we formalize the product-matching problem as generalized zero-shot multi-class classification following the definition in (Li et al., 2019). Let $\mathcal{O}$ denote the set of offers, and $\mathcal{P} = \mathcal{P}_s \cup \mathcal{P}_u$ the set of products consisting of two non-overlapping sets of seen products $\mathcal{P}_s$ and unseen products $\mathcal{P}_u$. Suppose we have three sets of data $\mathcal{D} = \{\mathcal{D}_s, \mathcal{D}_u, \mathcal{D}_a\}$, where $\mathcal{D}_s$, $\mathcal{D}_u$ and $\mathcal{D}_a$ are training, test and semantic description sets, respectively. The training and test sets consist of matching offer-product pairs, i.e., $\mathcal{D}_s = \{(o, p) : o \in \mathcal{O}, p \in \mathcal{P}_s\}$ and $\mathcal{D}_u = \{(o, p) : o \in \mathcal{O}, p \in \mathcal{P}\}$. The aim is to learn transferable knowledge from $\mathcal{D}_s$ to be able to predict matching products for offers present in pairs from $\mathcal{D}_u$ additionally making use of the semantic descriptions of offers and products $\mathcal{D}_a = \{\mathcal{O}, \mathcal{P}\}$.

Importantly, as this is a generalized zero-shot classification problem, not all products are observed in available training data. To be able to classify offers to products not observed during training, not only offers but also product classes need some representation.

Since the above definition of product matching is general and representation-agnostic, here we also formalize the specific settings of the product matching problem we solve in this work. We define each offer $o \in \mathcal{O}$ and each product $p \in \mathcal{P}$ as triples (t, a, c), where t is the title, a is the set of attributes and $c \in C$ is the category. The set of attributes a contains triples $(a_{name}, a_{values}, a_{unit})$, where a_{name} is the attribute name, a_{values} is a set of one or more values and a_{unit} is an optional unit. Titles of products or offers t, attribute names a_{name}, attribute values a_{values} and attribute units a_{unit} are strings possibly containing multiple words.

Given an offer $o = (t_o, a_o, c_o)$ the problem we tackle in this work is to find its matching product $p \in P$. In the classic product matching problem $P = \mathcal{P}$. Here, we consider a variant of this problem, where $P = \{p = (t_p, a_p, c_p) : p \in \mathcal{P}, c_o = c_p\}$, i.e., we only look for the matching product in a set of products that belong to the same category as the offer.

3   Product matching with similarity learning

In this work, we interpret the product matching problem as a similarity learning task. This approach allows us to cast product matching problem as a zero-shot learning problem, in result avoiding re-training the model on the introduction of new products or product categories.

3.1   Triplet loss objective

To solve the product matching problem with triplet loss (Hoffer and Ailon, 2015), we introduce a notion of similarity between offers and products, defined as proximity of their representations in some embedding space. Each training example is defined as a triplet (o, p^+, p^-), denoting an offer (anchor), a matching product (positive) and a non-matching product (negative). Given encoders $\mathcal{E}_\theta : \mathcal{O} \to \mathbf{R}^N$ and $\mathcal{E}_\phi : \mathcal{P} \to \mathbf{R}^N$, both transforming respective entities to vector representations in some embedding space (Section 3.3), and distance measure d (in our case the cosine distance), we adjust network parameters θ and ϕ to minimise the triplet loss objective:

$$\mathcal{L}(o, p^+, p^-) = max(0, m + d(\mathcal{E}_\theta(o), \mathcal{E}_\phi(p^+)) - d(\mathcal{E}_\theta(o), \mathcal{E}_\phi(p^-))),$$

where margin m is a hyperparameter. In this work we tie parameters of $\mathcal{E}_\theta$ and $\mathcal{E}_\phi$, employing a single instance of the encoder for both of them.

One shortcoming of the standard triplet loss objective is that majority of possible triplets prove trivial. To ensure that loss values do not vanish after the initial phase of training, a proper batch construction strategy is essential. Properly selected *active* (non-zero loss) triplets let one effectively evaluate and optimise the specified loss function (Section 3.4). The batch construction strategy will be an object of the ablation study.

3.2   Textual representation

The representation of each offer and product is a concatenated title, attributes values, and units, which is then lower-cased and pass into a fast byte-pair encoder (Sennrich et al., 2016). We also tested including descriptions and attributes names in the representation, but in all of our experiments, they deteriorate the model performance. We fit the tokenizer on our domain offer and product corpora with a vocabulary size of 30k tokens.

3.3   Encoder architectures

It is important in the similarity learning setting to properly choose the encoder architecture. Our main focus is the transformer (Vaswani et al., 2017) based encoders, which recently gained a lot of attention due to achieving state-of-the-art results on Natural Language Understanding benchmarks (Wang et al., 2018; Rybak et al., 2020). Our BERT usage as an encoder is inspired by (Reimers and Gurevych, 2019). We use a bag of words (BOW) embeddings model based on StarSpace (Wu et al., 2017b) as a simple baselines. The attention mechanism used in the transformer allows the model to learn the context and importance of words in an entity, whereas, in BOW embeddings, all of the words are treated equally and independently. Transformer architectures also allow the model to track the position of the words in a sequence, which we find beneficial in product matching task. To leverage our non-annotated data, we use the masked language model (MLM) pretraining objective described originally in the BERT paper (Devlin et al., 2019), but follow the improved training procedure from (Liu et al., 2019). We also explore scaling down the number of parameters with both the number of layers reduction and the knowledge distillation approach (Sanh et al., 2019). For our product matching downstream task, we finetune the standard BERT model with an additional layer of 768 linear units on top of the mean pooled last layer BERT activations which we call eComBERT in the rest of the paper.

3.4 Batch construction strategy

The metric learning training aims at embedding similar items closer to each other than to the dissimilar ones. This objective is not optimized directly, but via a surrogate like margin-based triplet loss on a batch of triplets. The strategy for choosing which triplets to include in a batch heavily impacts the learning curve and the final performance of the model. If the negatives are too distant compared to the positives, the triplet loss is zero, and such triplet does not contribute to the progress of training. If the negatives are too similar to the anchors or positives, the model may be trained on noise. In our setup, the anchors and positives are well defined, as they are offer and positive product pairs from a batch of matches. However, the choice of negatives in non-trivial. One option is to select the negatives uniformly at random (Wu et al., 2017b). In metric learning, plenty of other strategies for selecting triplets exist, for example, batch hard (Hermans et al., 2017), semi-hard (Schroff et al., 2015), or distance weighted sampling (Wu et al., 2017a). Those strategies are designed for anchors and positive and negative items coming from the same domain, which is not the case in our problem. For a well-structured overview of possible strategies, we refer the reader to (Musgrave et al., 2019).

In our setup the triplets batch construction begins with sampling a batch of matches used as the anchor-positive pairs in triplets. For negative item selection we consider three strategies. The simplest strategy is a modification of the random negative selection. It randomly selects a negative from the non-matching products in the category of the anchor. For the purpose of this work, we name it *category random* (CR) strategy.

The second explored approach is a modification of the batch hard strategy adjusted for our problem setup. The standard batch hard strategy, as proposed in (Hermans et al., 2017), starts with a batch of items from K classes, with N items per class. Then, to construct the batch of triplets, it uses each item as an anchor, and for each anchor selects the least similar matching (from the same class) item as the *hard positive* and the most similar mismatching item as the *hard negative*. As in our setup anchors and positive/negative items belong to different domains, we need to modify this strategy. As before, it starts with a batch of anchor-positive pairs and then selects the negative as the most similar product from all the non-matching products in the sampled batch of matches. We refer to this strategy as *batch hard* (BH) in the experiments. The performance of this strategy depends on the batch size, as the larger is batch, the harder negatives are likely to be found.

For the third batch construction method, we propose the *category hard* (CH) strategy. It is similar to the category random strategy, but instead of selecting the negative at random from the products in a given category, it selects the one that is most similar to the anchor offer. It requires embeddings of all products, which are time and resource consuming to obtain. However, as the model and the similarity of products does not change too fast, we recompute the embeddings every several, e.g. 100 or 500, updates. This value should be set to properly trade-off the time spent in embedding the products, and the mismatch of the current state of the model and used product embeddings.

4 Experiments and results

In this section we present our experimental results, focusing on different aspects of the training pipeline. After briefly introducing the datasets and the baselines, we show different trade-offs that cover both the architectural choices for the model, and the batch construction strategies.

4.1 Datasets

We perform all the experiments using proprietary datasets composed by offer-product matches originating from a real-world e-commerce application. We conduct all the experiments using three datasets: ELECTRONICS, BEAUTY, and CULTURE. The three datasets differ mainly in the number of products and their main statistics are shown in Table 1.

	Available matches	Products
CULTURE	300K	800K
ELECTRONICS	200K	400K
BEAUTY	300K	200K

Table 1: Datasets used for our experiments. For each dataset, we report the number of training matches and the number of products.

4.2 Training setup

We split the available matches into train (80%) and test (20%) sets. Unless specified differently, in all experiments the test set was generated in such a way that half of the products originated from $\mathcal{D}_u$, while the other half did not. This test set better emulates the generalized zero-shot multi-class classification scenario we are dealing with, i.e., users may create an offer whose matching product already exists in the product catalog, or not. A deeper analysis of the zero-shot performances of our model is provided in Section 4.7.

After separately pretraining the specific language model, we trained one encoder for each dataset. Unless differently stated, we run all the experiments training each model for 5000 steps, setting the batch size to 32 and Adam optimiser (Kingma and Ba, 2014), with initial learning rate set to $2 \cdot 10^{-5}$.

The main evaluation metric we report is accuracy (often referred to as ACC@1 in similarity learning literature), i.e., the fraction of correctly matched offers. In particular, we consider that an offer matches a product when, given an offer representation in the embedding space, the closest product representation in terms of cosine distance is indeed the matching product.

4.3 Baselines

We compare eComBERT against the following baselines:

- a modified implementation of the StarSpace (Wu et al., 2017c) BOW encoder, a commonly used neural embedding baseline for similarity learning problems,

- non-finetuned[1] HerBERT (Rybak et al., 2020) a BERT-based encoder pretrained in RoBERTa's fashion on a big Polish language corpus,

- finetuned HerBERT, with an additional 768 dimension linear layer on the top of mean pooled last layer BERT activations (see Section 3.3),

- non-finetuned eComBERT.

Since language-specific BERT models perform better than general-purpose English models (Rybak et al., 2020), we do not include the latter among the baselines. To make a fair comparison, we apply the CR strategy and objective as described in Section 3.1 for all the experiments.

	CULTURE	ELECTRONICS	BEAUTY
BOW	0.8863	0.8032	0.7687
HerBERT-NFT	0.8206	0.6716	0.5542
HerBERT	0.9550	0.8580	0.9064
eComBERT-NFT	0.8208	0.6755	0.6127
eComBERT	**0.9777**	**0.8840**	**0.9219**

Table 2: Test accuracy per each dataset. NFT stands for *non-finetuned*.

Results shown in Table 2 justify the application of more complex models such as BERT-based architecture over a simple BOW-based one for a product matching task. Moreover, we see how much we

---

[1]By *non-finetuned* we mean that we did not further train the weights of the encoder, but we used the mean pooled BERT last layer activations as embeddings for our entities.

improve pretrained BERT embeddings with our finetuning procedure. Finally, since the only difference between HerBERT and eComBERT is the corpus they were trained on, we conclude that pretraining the language model on a task-specific corpus (such as textual descriptions of offer and products in an e-commerce platform) leads to more accurate results.

4.4 Pretraining steps vs performance

Standard BERT model needs hundreds of thousands of update steps to converge and longer training generally translates into better downstream task performance. Since MLM objective is not strictly related to our product matching task, we check how the number of pretraining iterations affects the downstream task performance. Figure 1 shows text accuracy for the BEAUTY dataset for BERT models pretrained for a different number of steps. We see significant gains early on into pretraining, but after 20k steps into pretraining further optimization of the MLM objective does not translate into better downstream task performance, as model performance on product matching tasks fluctuates, even though MLM optimization does not converge. We have observed similar phenomena for different datasets and different BERT architectures and it suggests, that longer pretraining does not improve product matching performance.

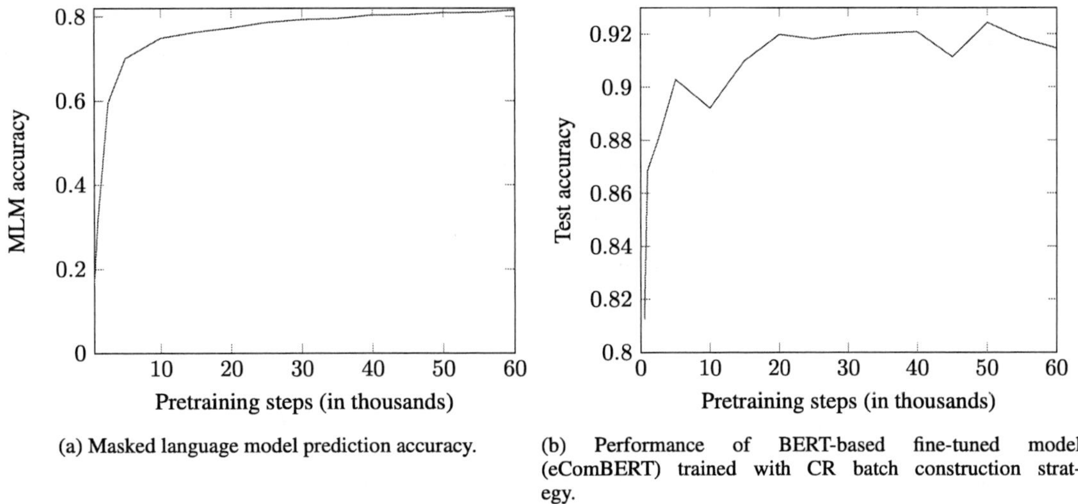

(a) Masked language model prediction accuracy.

(b) Performance of BERT-based fine-tuned model (eComBERT) trained with CR batch construction strategy.

Figure 1: Pre-training and downstream task model performance.

4.5 Batch construction strategy

We explore the impact of the sampling strategy on the fraction of active triplets and the performance of the finetuned models. Particularly, we experiment with the three batch construction strategies proposed in Section 3.4: category random, batch hard and category hard.

First, we investigate how the fraction of active triplets changes depending on how the batch is constructed. In Figure 2, we show the smoothed fraction of active triplets for BERT-based models in the initial phase of finetuning. In Figure 2a, we compare the batch construction strategies for the HerBERT model. In the very first steps of finetuning, BH leads to more active triplets than CR, but after around 50 steps those two strategies perform on par. The proposed CH strategy results in much more active triplets, with nearly all triplets being active in the beginning. Later, the fraction drops, and after the product embeddings are recomputed after the 100th step, it raises sharply. In the following stage of finetuning, we do not observe such sudden changes, since the model has already started to converge and there is no dramatic difference between subsequent recomputations of the embeddings.

Next, in Figure 2b we compare the active triplets fraction for two encoder architectures: eComBERT and HerBERT, both employing the CH strategy. Interestingly, in the initial 60 training steps training, the fraction of active triplets is higher for eComBERT than for HerBERT, while later the situation changes, and the HerBERT encoder consistently yields more active triplets. This may be caused by the fact that

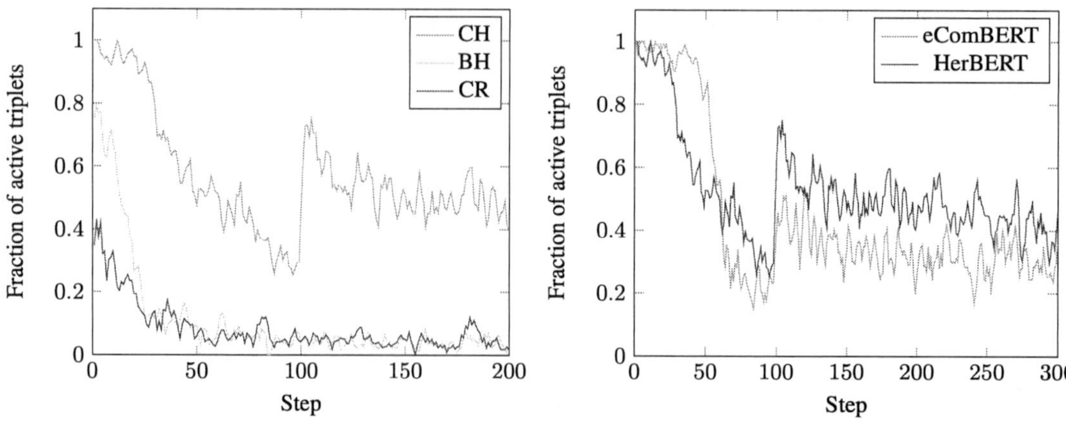

(a) Active triplet fraction for HerBERT initialised model for different negative item selection strategies.

(b) Active triplet fraction for HerBERT and eComBERT initialised model for category hard strategy.

Figure 2: Fraction of active triplets in the initial steps of training for BERT based models on ELECTRONICS dataset. Note: CH was run recomputing products' embeddings every 100 steps.

eComBERT better understands the e-commerce domain and places similar items closer to each other from the very beginning. HerBERT is a general model, and may not understand the similarity of product and offers well. In the later training steps HerBERT yields more active triplets than eComBERT as it yields worse training and test accuracy.

Finally, in Table 3 we report the test accuracy for HerBERT and eComBERT and different batch construction strategies. After 1000 steps the models are not yet converged, but it is already known which strategy gives the best performing model. First, we see that for HerBERT and eComBERT initialized models, the category hard strategy gives the highest accuracy, and the e-commerce eComBERT initialized model performs better. Secondly, we see that the models perform similarly for either batch hard or category random strategy, as those strategies produce little active triplets that may contribute to the change of the model. For the same reason, eComBERT trained with category random or batch hard strategy outperforms HerBERT with those strategies: eComBERT was a stronger model in the beginning, and the models have not changed much during training.

	category random	batch hard	category hard
HerBERT	0.8340	0.8352	0.9096
eComBERT	0.8803	0.8790	**0.9270**

Table 3: Test accuracy of models trained with different strategies for 1000 steps on ELECTRONICS.

4.6 Encoder architectures

BERT pretraining is very costly and its inference time is quite substantial in comparison to simpler models. To alleviate those issues, we ran eComBERT pretraining with 4 BERT layers (small eComBERT) and we pretrained DistilBERT on our own internal data (Distil eComBERT). In Table 4 we report test accuracies for the models on all of our prepared datasets. Those models still achieve competitive results across different domains, when cutting the inference time by half and two thirds, for Distil eComBERT and small eComBERT, respectively.

4.7 Zero-shot performance

In this section, we evaluate the zero-shot performance of our best eComBERT model against the BOW-based model and eComBERT without fine-tuning. To properly compare the performance, we prepare a separate dataset, where the test set consists only of products not seen in training. We use CH batch

	ELECTRONICS	BEAUTY	CULTURE
eComBERT	**0.9429**	**0.9674**	**0.9873**
Distil eComBERT	0.9410	0.9666	**0.9873**
small eComBERT	0.9400	0.9656	0.9865

Table 4: Accuracy of models with different BERT architectures trained for 5k steps with category hard sampling strategy.

construction and standard training procedure as discussed previously. To avoid leakage, we exclude test products from sampling. We report training and test accuracy in table 5. Based on those results, we conclude that the BOW model is not complex enough to overfit the training data and we observe similar results both on training and test data. Moreover, we see how much we improve pretrained embeddings with our finetuning procedure. After 5k update steps BERT starts to overfit to the data, while still generalizing fairly well on D_u.

	Training accuracy	Zero-shot accuracy
BOW	0.7929	0.8016
eComBERT-NFT	0.6519	0.6656
eComBERT	0.9086	**0.8873**

Table 5: Zero-shot performance of models trained for 5k steps using CH batch construction strategy on ELECTRONICS dataset.

5 Related work

E-commerce is inherently bound to products, and many challenges of this area are related to them. Such challenges include product entity resolution. Product entity resolution task is not well defined, and it is often formulated as one of the following problems: understanding which items from various sources (e.g. e-commerce platforms) correspond to the same real-world entity, i.e., a product (Li et al., 2020a; Fu et al., 2019); understanding which items (e.g. offers) from a single platform correspond to the same real-world entity (Shah et al., 2018). Last but not least, products and offers have normally multi-modal representations, i.e., they may be described by partially structured text and images at the same time. The way such representations are used when extracting information is a design choice, that highly influences the chosen algorithms and prepossessing strategies.

The former problem, product entity resolution of items from various sources, usually requires not only text matching but also understanding differently structured textual information. To this end, many solutions were proposed. Here we only mention works that use specific language models (Fu et al., 2019); that apply different machine translation techniques (Li et al., 2018), or other methods for comparison of attributes and titles (Li et al., 2020a). For more references related to this problem, we refer the reader to (Ristoski et al., 2018; Fu et al., 2019; Li et al., 2020a).

The latter problem, product matching, i.e., product entity resolution among items from a single platform, normally includes matching the item to a product defined in some product catalog. Such a problem was considered by (Shah et al., 2018), which compares two approaches to solve this task: classification based on fastText-based (Joulin et al., 2017) features; and similarity learning using BiLSTM neural network trained with contrastive loss. Many other case studies of this problem exist, for example (More, 2017), which describes a combination of learned similarities of texts and images neural networks.

6 Conclusions

In this work, we leverage the transformer architecture combined with the similarity learning approach to solve the product matching task in e-commerce. We show that finetuning even general-purpose transformers yields models that perform significantly better than other similarity learning baselines such as

StarSpace. These models can be further improved by employing BERT models pretrained on domain-specific data. Our experiments emphasize the importance of the employed batch construction strategy. Particularly, in our specific problem setup, a tailored batch construction strategy called *category hard* proved to significantly improve the percentage of active triplets and consequently the model performance.

One particular challenge that we encountered during our work with the product matching problem, and one which we believe has not been adequately addressed in the product matching literature is concept drift. This problem, also called covariate shift or nonstationarity, refers to the change in the relationship between input and output variables over time. In the case of product matching, it ultimately leads to a gradual drop in accuracy of the predicted product matches. Apart from the degradation of the model performance, another important issue arising from concept drift is the difficulty of evaluating new model versions. For a stationary problem, the standard procedure involves preparing a potentially costly human-annotated dataset once and using it for comparing the subsequent model version. Unfortunately, this is not a viable strategy if the test set cannot be fixed. We plan to investigate the concept drift problem in our future work.

References

Ursin Brunner and Kurt Stockinger. 2019. Entity matching on unstructured data: an active learning approach. In *2019 6th Swiss Conference on Data Science (SDS)*, pages 97–102. IEEE.

Ursin Brunner and Kurt Stockinger. 2020. Entity matching with transformer architectures - A step forward in data integration. In *Advances in Database Technology - EDBT*, volume 2020-March, pages 463–473.

Jacob Devlin, Ming-Wei Chang, Kenton Lee, and Kristina Toutanova. 2019. BERT: Pre-training of deep bidirectional transformers for language understanding. In *Proceedings of the 2019 Conference of the North American Chapter of the Association for Computational Linguistics: Human Language Technologies, Volume 1 (Long and Short Papers)*, pages 4171–4186, Minneapolis, Minnesota, June. Association for Computational Linguistics.

Cheng Fu, Xianpei Han, Le Sun, Bo Chen, Wei Zhang, Suhui Wu, and Hao Kong. 2019. End-to-End Multi-Perspective Matching for Entity Resolution. In *Proceedings of the Twenty-Eighth International Joint Conference on Artificial Intelligence, {IJCAI-19}*, pages 4961–4967. International Joint Conferences on Artificial Intelligence Organization.

Alexander Hermans, Lucas Beyer, and Bastian Leibe. 2017. In defense of the triplet loss for person re-identification. *CoRR*, abs/1703.07737.

Elad Hoffer and Nir Ailon. 2015. Deep metric learning using triplet network. In *International Workshop on Similarity-Based Pattern Recognition*, pages 84–92. Springer.

Armand Joulin, Edouard Grave, Piotr Bojanowski, and Tomas Mikolov. 2017. Bag of tricks for efficient text classification. In *Proceedings of the 15th Conference of the European Chapter of the Association for Computational Linguistics: Volume 2, Short Papers*, pages 427–431, Valencia, Spain, April. Association for Computational Linguistics.

Diederik P. Kingma and Jimmy Ba. 2014. Adam: A method for stochastic optimization. cite arxiv:1412.6980Comment: Published as a conference paper at the 3rd International Conference for Learning Representations, San Diego, 2015.

Pradap Konda, Sanjib Das, Paul Suganthan GC, AnHai Doan, Adel Ardalan, Jeffrey R Ballard, Han Li, Fatemah Panahi, Haojun Zhang, Jeff Naughton, et al. 2016. Magellan: Toward building entity matching management systems. *Proceedings of the VLDB Endowment*, 9(12):1197–1208.

Hanna Köpcke, Andreas Thor, and Erhard Rahm. 2010. Evaluation of entity resolution approaches on real-world match problems. *Proceedings of the VLDB Endowment*, 3(1-2):484–493.

Maggie Yundi Li, Stanley Kok, and Liling Tan. 2018. Don't classify, translate: Multi-level e-commerce product categorization via machine translation. *arXiv preprint arXiv:1812.05774*.

Kai Li, Martin Renqiang Min, and Yun Fu. 2019. Rethinking zero-shot learning: A conditional visual classification perspective. In *Proceedings of the IEEE International Conference on Computer Vision*, pages 3583–3592.

Juan Li, Zhicheng Dou Dou, Yutao Zhu, and Ji-Rong Wen Zuo, Xiaochen Wen. 2020a. Deep cross-platform product matching in e-commerce. *Information Retrieval Journal*, 23(2):136–158.

Yuliang Li, Jinfeng Li, Yoshihiko Suhara, AnHai Doan, and Wang-Chiew Tan. 2020b. Deep entity matching with pre-trained language models. *arXiv preprint arXiv:2004.00584*.

Yinhan Liu, Myle Ott, Naman Goyal, Jingfei Du, Mandar Joshi, Danqi Chen, Omer Levy, Mike Lewis, Luke Zettlemoyer, and Veselin Stoyanov. 2019. Roberta: A robustly optimized bert pretraining approach. *arXiv preprint arXiv:1907.11692*.

Ajinkya More. 2017. Product matching in ecommerce using deep learning. https://medium.com/walmartlabs/product-matching-in-ecommerce-4f19b6aebaca.

Kevin Musgrave, Ser-Nam Lim, and Serge Belongie. 2019. Pytorch metric learning. https://github.com/KevinMusgrave/pytorch-metric-learning.

Nils Reimers and Iryna Gurevych. 2019. Sentence-bert: Sentence embeddings using siamese bert-networks. In *EMNLP/IJCNLP*.

Petar Ristoski, Petar Petrovski, Peter Mika, and Heiko Paulheim. 2018. A machine learning approach for product matching and categorization. *Semantic Web*, 9:707–728.

Piotr Rybak, Robert Mroczkowski, Janusz Tracz, and Ireneusz Gawlik. 2020. KLEJ: Comprehensive benchmark for polish language understanding. In *Proceedings of the 58th Annual Meeting of the Association for Computational Linguistics*, pages 1191–1201, Online, July. Association for Computational Linguistics.

Victor Sanh, Lysandre Debut, Julien Chaumond, and Thomas Wolf. 2019. Distilbert, a distilled version of bert: smaller, faster, cheaper and lighter. *arXiv preprint arXiv:1910.01108*.

Florian Schroff, Dmitry Kalenichenko, and James Philbin. 2015. Facenet: A unified embedding for face recognition and clustering. *CoRR*, abs/1503.03832.

Rico Sennrich, Barry Haddow, and Alexandra Birch. 2016. Neural machine translation of rare words with subword units. In *Proceedings of the 54th Annual Meeting of the Association for Computational Linguistics (Volume 1: Long Papers)*, pages 1715–1725, Berlin, Germany, August. Association for Computational Linguistics.

Kashif Shah, Selcuk Kopru, and Jean-David Ruvini. 2018. Neural network based extreme classification and similarity models for product matching. In *Proceedings of the 2018 Conference of the North American Chapter of the Association for Computational Linguistics: Human Language Technologies, Volume 3 (Industry Papers)*, pages 8–15, New Orleans - Louisiana, jun. Association for Computational Linguistics.

Andreas Thor. 2010. Toward an adaptive string similarity measure for matching product offers. *INFORMATIK 2010. Service Science–Neue Perspektiven für die Informatik. Band 1*.

Ashish Vaswani, Noam Shazeer, Niki Parmar, Jakob Uszkoreit, Llion Jones, Aidan N Gomez, Łukasz Kaiser, and Illia Polosukhin. 2017. Attention is all you need. In *Advances in neural information processing systems*, pages 5998–6008.

Alex Wang, Amanpreet Singh, Julian Michael, Felix Hill, Omer Levy, and Samuel R Bowman. 2018. Glue: A multi-task benchmark and analysis platform for natural language understanding. *arXiv preprint arXiv:1804.07461*.

Chao-Yuan Wu, R. Manmatha, Alexander J. Smola, and Philipp Krähenbühl. 2017a. Sampling matters in deep embedding learning. *CoRR*, abs/1706.07567.

L. Wu, A. Fisch, S. Chopra, K. Adams, A. Bordes, and J. Weston. 2017b. Starspace: Embed all the things! *arXiv preprint arXiv:1709.03856*.

Ledell Wu, Adam Fisch, Sumit Chopra, Keith Adams, Antoine Bordes, and Jason Weston. 2017c. Starspace: Embed all the things! *CoRR*, abs/1709.03856.

Aspect-Similarity-Aware Historical Influence Modeling
for Rating Prediction

Ryo Shimura   Shotaro Misawa   Masahiro Sato
Tomoki Taniguchi   Tomoko Ohkuma
Fuji Xerox Co., Ltd.
{shimura.ryo,misawa.shotaro,masahiro.sato,
taniguchi.tomoki,ohkuma.tomoko}@fujixerox.co.jp

Abstract

Many e-commerce services provide customer review systems. Previous laboratory studies have indicated that the ratings recorded by these systems differ from the actual evaluations of the users, owing to the influence of historical ratings in the system. Some studies have proposed using real-world datasets to model rating prediction. Herein, we propose an aspect-similarity-aware historical influence model for rating prediction using natural language processing techniques. In general, each user provides a rating considering different aspects. Thus, it can be assumed that historical ratings provided considering similar aspects to those of later ones will influence evaluations of users more. By focusing on the review-topic similarities, we show that our method predicts ratings more accurately than the previous historical-inference-aware model. In addition, we examine whether our model can predict "intrinsic rating," which is given if users were not influenced by historical ratings. We performed an intrinsic rating prediction task, and showed that our model achieved improved performance. Our method can be useful to debias user ratings collected by customer review systems. The debiased ratings help users to make decision properly and systems to provide helpful recommendations. This might improve the user experience of e-commerce services.

1 Introduction

Currently, many e-commerce services like Amazon provide customer review systems (CRS). CRSs retrieve user feedbacks, which contain mainly ratings and reviews, shared across entire users, enabling (1) subsequent users to help decide whether to purchase the items and (2) the systems to make recommendations for items.

Previous studies have shown that historical ratings presented by a CRS can create historical influence (Adomavicius et al., 2016). In this study, "historical influence" refers to a phenomena that historical ratings make users give ratings apart from their natural evaluation. According to the previous work, users tend to give higher ratings to items presented with a high average historical rating. Such influence affects the unbiased purchase decisions of subsequent users, and provides inaccurate and unhelpful recommendations. Therefore, it is important that the recommender system estimates the "intrinsic rating", which is given if users were not influenced. Recently, some studies have proposed historical-influence-aware rating prediction models (Wang et al., 2014; Liu et al., 2016; Zhang et al., 2019). In particular, Zhang et al. (2019) found that the subsequent rating of an item correlates with the average historical ratings at the time of evaluation. They concluded that such correlation patterns could be described by an assimilation-contrast theory (Anderson, 1973). Subsequent users tend to provide ratings according to the average historical rating when it is close to their intrinsic ratings (assimilation); conversely, they provide ratings against the average historical rating when it differs from their intrinsic ratings (contrast). The proposed model is called the historical-influence-aware latent factor (HIALF) model, and it has achieved significant improvements in rating prediction. In addition, the model can be used to estimate intrinsic ratings.

Proceedings of the Workshop on Natural Language Processing in E-Commerce (EComNLP), pages 76–86
Barcelona, Spain (Online), Dec 12, 2020.

We assume that evaluators are influenced significantly by the historical ratings given under aspects similar to theirs. In general, different users focus on different aspects of an item and the rating is given based on these aspects. For example, a user concerned more about the color of an item may provide a different rating for the item than a user concerned more about the price. Therefore, it is natural that the strength of the influence from each historical rating depends on the aspects under which the rating was provided. Consequently, evaluators are likely to provide ratings higher or lower than intrinsic ratings, when the historical rating is high or low, respectively.

In this paper, we conduct preliminary analyses to confirm that our assumption is appropriate. Then, we propose an aspect-aware historical influence model for rating prediction using natural language processing techniques (Figure 1 (A)). We apply topic modeling to extract aspects from reviews, and calculate the similarities in the aspects. The calculated aspect similarity is used to weight the corresponding historical ratings. The weighted ratings are then aggregated to integrate the matrix factorization (MF) model (Koren et al., 2009). We conduct experiments to show that our model outperforms HIALF and MF in rating prediction on four real-world datasets. Additionally, to examine whether our model can predict intrinsic ratings, we evaluate our model on the additional task of predicting the first rating for each item. Our results demonstrate that the proposed model predict the intrinsic ratings of users accurately.

Contributions: The contributions of this work are summarized as follows.

- We develop an aspect-similarity-aware historical influence model using reviews.

- We show that our model can estimate the intrinsic ratings of users more accurately.

- Our results indicate that users are strongly influenced by the historical ratings provided under aspects similar to theirs.

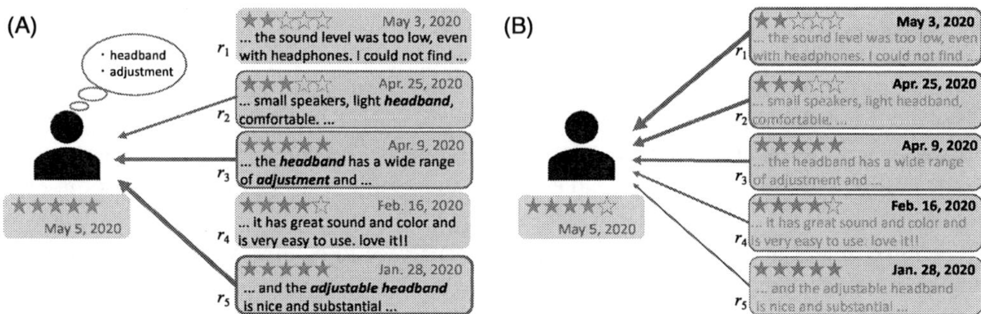

Figure 1: Illustration of historical influence models. A user purchased headphones and rated it. (A) Model where users are influenced by ratings whose review was written under aspects similar to those of the evaluator (B) Model where users are influcnccd more by recent ratings used in HIALF. For example, in illustration (A), evaluator u focuses on the "headband" and "adjustment" of the item. Thus, the evaluator will be influenced significantly by ratings r_2, r_3 and r_5, because their reviews mention "headband" and "adjustment" of the item.

2   Related Works

Laboratory experiment on historical influence: Adomavicius et al. (2016) showed that users may fail to evaluate an item properly when they preliminarily observe system-predicted or averaged ratings. For example, even when comparing items of the same quality, users tend to give higher ratings to the one presented with a higher average historical rating.

Modeling historical influence: Some studies have modeled historical influence in real-world datasets (Wang et al., 2014; Liu et al., 2016; Zhang et al., 2019). Wang et al. (2014) developed Herding Effect Aware Rating Dynamics Model (HEARD) introducing generative model. Although the model calculates the distribution of next rating from historical ratings to model dynamics of rating growth, it does not take user preference into account. By contrast, Liu et al. (2016) and Zhang et al. (2019) attempted to model influence from historical ratings on subsequent users combining with MF. Liu et al. preliminarily analyzed the real-world datasets and found that the next rating correlates with the average of the historical ratings of the item. Then, they proposed the model which has the term considering the average and number of historical ratings. Similarly, Zhang et al. analyzed the other datasets and concluded that such correlation patterns can be explained by "Assimilate-Contrast" theory in psychology, based on which they developed HIALF and showed that the model outperforms previous methods. Although these methods have considered historical influence, they ignore reviews. Our model is on top of these works, and our proposed method uses reviews to model aspect-similarity-aware historical influence.

Rating prediction with reviews: Many works use reviews to improve accuracy, in particular, some of them utilize the MF model (McAuley and Leskovec, 2013; Ling et al., 2014; Tan et al., 2016; Zheng et al., 2017; Chen et al., 2018; Li et al., 2019b). They differ from our work in using reviews to model user-preferences and item-features. Our method utilizes reviews not for user/item modeling directly, but for modeling historical influence.

Modeling social influence: Recent works have studied social influence, which is another type of influence on evaluation (Ye et al., 2012; Guo et al., 2014; Li et al., 2019a; Li et al., 2019b; Wu et al., 2019a; Wu et al., 2019b). These works model social influence under explicit user-user networks such as friends, and trust. However, some of CRSs like Amazon does not have explicit network. Mukherjee and Guennemann (2019) proposed the model GhostLink, which can infer implicit user-user network from only timestamped reviews of the users. GhostLink use echoed/copied topics of reviews as an indication of influence. They showed that they can predict ratings accurately using the inferred influence network. There is a difference that while we focus on the historical influence from ratings and reviews, GhostLink is motivated to infer the user-user networks to find out who-influences-whom relationships.

3   Preliminary Analysis

Zhang et al. (2019) investigated the relationship between subsequent ratings and historical ratings at the point of each evaluation. If users provide completely uninfluenced feedbacks, there should be no correlation between subsequent ratings and historical ratings. They obtained relationships between the subsequent rating and historical ratings, and evaluated the relationships using the slopes of fitted lines in the points obtained. This is discussed in detail in Section 3.2.

Following Zhang et al., we performed preliminary analyses to confirm that users are influenced by the ratings of user feedback considering similar aspects. Specifically, we use restricted subsets of user feedbacks for averaging, instead of subsets of all historical ratings as in the study of Zhang et al. Each subset is formulated to have similar aspects for each target user feedback. Then, we plot the target ratings against the average of the subsets. Lastly, we compare the slopes of the fitted lines, and examine whether these slopes change depending on the subset used for averaging.

3.1   Datasets

We used four datasets of different categories from the Amazon dataset (He and McAuley, 2016). These datasets include reviews and ratings from May 1996 to July 2014. From these datasets, we extracted user IDs, item IDs, 1-5-star(s) ratings, free-text reviews, and timestamps. The statistics of the datasets are summarized in Table 1.

	# items	# users	# ratings&reviews
Movies and TVs	208,321	2,088,620	4,607,047
Electronics	498,196	4,261,096	7,824,482
Clothing, Shoes and Jewelry	1,503,384	3,117,268	5,748,920
Books	2,370,585	8,026,324	2,507,155

Table 1: Summary of the Amazon datasets.

3.2 Measurement Procedure

First, we describe the details of the analyses conducted by Zhang et al. Items with overall average ratings in the range of 2.9 to 3.1 were used. A prior expectation $e_{i,n}$ is calculated as

$$e_{i,n} = \frac{1}{|\mathcal{H}_{i,n}|} \sum_{r \in \mathcal{H}_{i,n}} r, \tag{1}$$

where $\mathcal{H}_{i,n}$ denotes the historical ratings of $r_{i,n}$: $\{r_{i,1}, r_{i,2}, \ldots, r_{i,n-2}, r_{i,n-1}\}$. The prior expectations are rounded off to one decimal place. For the set of the pairs of $(r_{i,n}, e_{i,n})$, a binning operation is performed by each $e_{i,n}$. As a result, we obtain bins of $\{1.0, 1.1, \ldots, 4.9, 5.0\}$, and each bin contains a set of the next ratings $\{\dot{r}_1, \ldots, \dot{r}_{N_e}\}$ given by different users under a prior expectation e. These next ratings are averaged within each bin of the prior expectation e as

$$\bar{r}_e = \frac{1}{N_e} \sum_{k=1}^{N_e} \dot{r}_k, \tag{2}$$

where N_e denotes the number of next ratings contained in the bin of the prior expectation e. Finally, the prior expectations e and average next ratings $\bar{r}_e$ are plotted, and the Pearson correlation coefficient and slopes of the fitted lines are calculated. A linear regression model is used for the fitting.

In the original procedure, all historical ratings of $r_{i,n}$ are used (Eq. 1). Here, we consider using subsets for calculating the prior expectations, instead of using $\mathcal{H}_{i,n}$. We adopt the following factors to extract subsets for each user feedback:

- *Random*: Randomly selecting ten user feedbacks.

- *Sentence-Similarity*: Selecting the ten most similar user feedbacks. We use the bag-of-words of TF-IDF to measure sentence similarity for simplicity.

An issue of concern is that some undesirable positive correlations may occur in cases where the target reviews contain words, such as "good," "great," "bad," and "terrible," that directly express the quality of the item. In these cases, the user feedback extracted based on similarity also contains such words, and has positive correlations. However, these are not derived from historical influence.

Consider this, we also apply the same procedure for the future ratings of $r_{i,n}$. The analyses using future ratings are expected to capture only positive correlations that are not related to historical influences. Therefore, by *subtracting* the effects of the future ratings from those of the historical ratings, we can measure the historical influence from each subset without undesirable positive correlations. In future ratings analyses, we extract ratings from $\{r_{i,n+1}, r_{i,n+2}, \ldots, r_{i,N_i}\}$ for a target rating $r_{i,n}$, where N_i denotes the number of ratings of an item i in the datasets.

3.3 Results

In Table 2, we compared the Pearson correlation coefficients and slopes for each factor. To avoid noise owing to the low sample size, we fitted lines to the points with prior experiments in range of 2.0 to 4.0. There were strong positive coefficients for the *Sentence-Similarity* in four datasets in both the historical and future ratings analyses. This indicates that linear regression is well-fitted. A comparison of the slopes shows that *Random* exhibits mostly flat slopes for both the historical and future rating analyses on the four datasets. By contrast, *Sentence-Similarity* exhibits positive slopes.

Sentence-Similarity exhibited high slopes on the four datasets in the historical-ratings analyses; conversely, the slopes decreased in the future ratings analyses. This implies that there may be cases where the target reviews contain words expressing quality, as discussed previously. However, the slopes of the historical-ratings analyses are higher than those of the future-ratings analyses. Therefore, we concluded that *Sentence-Similarity*, which includes aspects similarity, might actually relate to the historical influence.

	Slope		Pearson Correction Coefficient	
	Random	*Sentence-Similarity*	*Random*	*Sentence-Similarity*
Movies	0.037 (0.013)	0.718 (0.428)	0.502 (0.176)	0.997 (0.995)
Electronics	-0.028 (-0.042)	0.763 (0.665)	0.422 (0.771)	0.997 (0.996)
Clothing	-0.093 (-0.116)	0.629 (0.531)	0.752 (0.874)	0.987 (0.983)
Books	-0.037 (-0.018)	0.549 (0.407)	0.398 (0.197)	0.995 (0.989

Table 2: Results of the historical-ratings (Upper lines) and future-ratings (Lower lines, within parentheses) analyses.

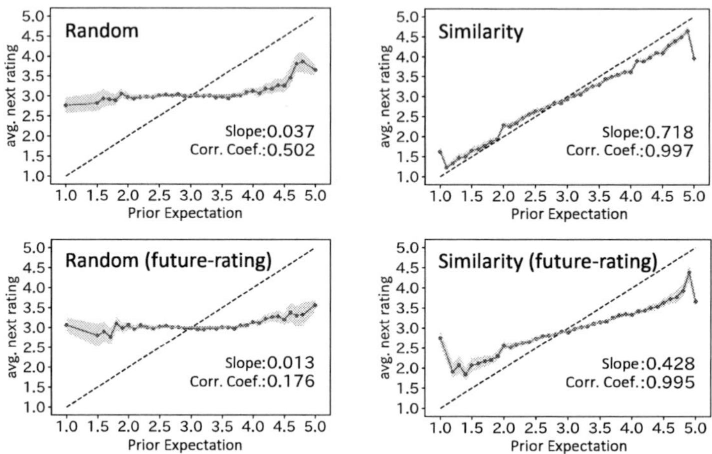

Figure 2: Plot of the prior expectations and average of next ratings in the Movies&TVs dataset. The x-axis represents the bins of prior expectation, and the y-axis represents the average of the next ratings.

4 Base Models

4.1 Biased Matrix Factorization Model

The biased MF model proposed by Koren et al. (2009) calculates an interaction between a user preference and an item feature as

$$\hat{r}_{u,i}^{\mathrm{MF}} = \mu + b_u + b_i + p_u^{\top} q_i. \tag{3}$$

Here, μ, b_u, and b_i denote the overall average, user bias, and item bias, respectively. p_u and q_i represent the l-dimensional user preference vector and item feature vector, respectively. This model has been widely used in rating prediction.

4.2 Historical Influence Aware Latent Factor Model

HIALF (Zhang et al., 2019) is designed under the assumption that the quality perceived by the users and prior expectations primarily form their ratings. The experienced quality represents the intrinsic evaluation of the users for item[1]. Prior expectation is defined as the average of the historical ratings that users observe prior to evaluation. Zhang et al. showed that user ratings tend to differ from the experienced quality because of being influenced. This indicates that the difference between the quality experienced by users and prior expectation is a signal of being influenced. Thus, user ratings will be

---

[1]Note that the "experienced quality" and "intrinsic rating" are different in this paper. $s_{u,i}$ in Eq. 4 denotes the former, which is defined in Zhang et al. (2019). The later is denoted by $b_u + s_{u,i}$ in this paper.

expressed as the sum of the experienced quality and influence based on this difference. HIALF predicts the n-th rating of i by u as:

$$r_{u,i,n}^{\text{HIALF}} = \underbrace{b_u + s_{u,i}}_{\text{MF}} + \underbrace{\alpha_u f\left(|\mathcal{H}_{i,n}|\right) \beta\left(e_{i,n} - s_{u,i}\right)}_{\text{Historical influence}}. \tag{4}$$

Here, $s_{u,i}$ and $e_{i,n}$ denote the experienced quality and prior expectation, α_u denotes the likelihood of a user u being influenced, and $\mathcal{H}_{i,n}$ denotes the set of historical ratings before u provided the rating $r_{i,n}$. The experienced quality is calculated as $s_{u,i} = \hat{r}_{u,i}^{\text{MF}} - b_u$. The prior expectation $e_{i,n}$ is calculated by the recency-weighted average of historical ratings as:

$$e_{i,n} = \frac{\sum_{k=1}^{n-1} \xi(n-k) \cdot r_{i,k}}{\sum_{k=1}^{n-1} \xi(n-k)}, \text{ where } \xi(d) = \exp(-\gamma * d). \tag{5}$$

The weights of each historical rating increase depending on the recency. This is based on the idea that users will focus more on recent historical ratings. In fact, Zhang et al. showed that the recency-weighted average is better than the uniform average.

Function $f(m)$ is sigmoid-form function modeling the magnifying impact of historical ratings with the size m as:

$$f(m) = \frac{a}{1 + \exp\left(-bm\right)} - \frac{a}{2}, \tag{6}$$

where m denotes the size of the historical ratings, and a, b are the learning parameters. The overall effect of the historical influence will be strong when m is large.

Function $\beta(x)$ is a bias curve representing the assimilate-contrast effect of $x = e_{i,n} - s_{u,i}$. Non-parametric kernel regression is used to fit a set of samples $\{(g_l, v_l)\}_{l=1}^{L}$ as:

$$\beta(x) = \frac{\sum_{l=1}^{L} w\left(x, g_l\right) \cdot v_l}{\sum_{l=1}^{L} w\left(x, g_l\right)}, \text{ where } w(x, g_l) = \exp\left(-\kappa \left(x - g_l\right)^2\right). \tag{7}$$

Here, $\{g_1, g_2, \ldots, g_{L-1}, g_L\}$ are fixed to $\{-4, -3.5, \ldots, 3.5, 4.0\}$ in order, and $\{v_1, \ldots, v_L\}$ are the learning parameters. κ is a hyperparameter controlling the smoothness of the function. The learned curve is expected to be formed as $\beta(x)$ grows where $|x|$ is small (assimilation); otherwise, it declines (contrast).

The original MF model (Eq. 3) cannot discriminate whether a high rating is due to the intrinsic rating or historical influence. By introducing the historical influence term, the MF term in HIALF can learn intrinsic features apart from historical influence.

5 Proposed Model

We propose the model under the assumption that the strength of the historical influence depends on aspects similarity between an evaluator and users who gave historical ratings. We use a topic model to vectorize the review, and the extracted topic is regarded as an aspect of the review. Then, we calculate the similarity between the review topics of the evaluator and those of the historical users. We use this similarity as the aspect similarity, because user reviews are considered to reflect their aspects. By considering aspect similarity, the proposed method is expected to model the historical influence accurately.

Our model is an extension of HIALF. The major difference lies in the calculation of prior expectation. In HIALF, the historical ratings and recency are used in the calculation. By contrast, the proposed model uses historical ratings and review topics. Concretely, we calculate the aspect similarity between the evaluator and each historical user, and then, the prior expectation only among the ratings with high aspect similarities. The model is described as follows:

$$\hat{r}_{u,i} = b_u + s_{u,i} + \alpha_u f\left(|\mathcal{H}_{i,n}|\right) \beta(e_{u,i}^{\text{simi}} - s_{u,i}). \tag{8}$$

Here, α_u represents the likelihood of the user u being influenced, and function $f(\cdot)$ and $\beta(\cdot)$ models the magnifying effect and the bias curve following HIALF, respectively (Eq. 6, 7). $e_{u,i}^{\text{simi}}$ denotes the aspect-aware prior expectation using the review-topic similarity. We detail the method in the following subsection.

5.1 Aspect-aware Prior Expectation

We introduce similarity-weighted aggregation method. To calculate the aspect-aware prior expectation $e_{u,i}^{\text{simi}}$, we extract top-k similar reviews and aggregate them as:

$$e_{u,i}^{\text{simi}} = \frac{\sum_{(d',r')\in\mathcal{D}_k^{\text{simi}}} r'\,\text{simi}^w(d',d_{u,i})}{\sum_{(d',r')\in\mathcal{D}_k^{\text{simi}}} \text{simi}^w(d',d_{u,i})}, \tag{9}$$

where $\mathcal{D}_k^{\text{simi}}$ denotes the subset of pairs of top-k similar review-topics vectors and corresponding ratings, w denotes scaling factor of similarity weighting, and $d_{u,i}$ denote the review-topics vector for item i by user u, respectively. In our paper, Latent Dirichlet Allocation (LDA) (Blei et al., 2003) is used for topic modeling and cosine similarity is used for similarity calculation. The prior expectation is designed to give large weight to historical ratings which seem to be given under similar aspects.

5.2 Objective Function

To learn the model, we define objective function as:

$$\mathcal{L}(\Theta) = \sum_{(u,i)\in\mathcal{T}} (r_{u,i} - \hat{r}_{u,i})^2 + \lambda_l(\|p_u\|^2 + \|q_i\|^2 + b_u^2 + b_i^2) + \lambda_\alpha \alpha_u^2 + \lambda_f(a^2 + b^2) + \lambda_\beta \left(\sum_{l=1}^{L} v_l^2\right). \tag{10}$$

Here, Θ denotes the learning parameters $p_u, q_i, b_u, b_i, \alpha_u, a, b$, and $\lambda_l, \lambda_\alpha, \lambda_f, \lambda_\beta$ are regularization hyperparameters for Θ. $\mathcal{T}$ denotes the set of user-item pairs in training data, and $r_{u,i}$ is the ground truth of the rating of item i by user u.

6 Experiments

We conducted two tasks: ordinay rating prediction (*Task 1*) and intrinsic rating prediction (*Task 2*). *Task 1* is widely used to evaluate recommender systems. In *Task 1*, we investigated the effect of top-k and w in Eq. 9. *Task 2* is where a model predicts the first ratings of every item. The first ratings can be used as the ground truth for the intrinsic ratings of users, because users who provided the first rating were not exposed to any historical influence. In *Task 2*, the ratings are predicted only from pre-trained users or item-features. The models are evaluated based on the ability to distinguish intrinsic ratings from historical influence. If a model successfully learns the intrinsic user-features, it will be able to accurately estimate the intrinsic ratings of users.

6.1 Experimental Settings

Dataset preprocessing: We preprocessed the four datasets described in Section 3. We preprocessed the datasets following (Zhang et al., 2019). We started by removing items with less than 75 ratings. Then, we extracted users with less than 50 ratings, and merged them into one *pseudo-user*. The pseudo-user is treated in the same manner as other users. This process aims to remove users whose data are too small to learn latent factors without reducing the historical ratings. The statistics of the preprocessed datasets are summarized in Table 3.

	# items	# users	# ratings&reviews
Movies and TV	11,194	2,311	3,079,522
Electronics	17,727	400	4,860,410
Clothing, Shoes and Jewelry	9,623	2	1,677,798
Books	42,462	9,401	9,321,929

Table 3: Summary of the statistics of preprocessed datasets.

Baseline models: We compared our model with the following baseline models in *Task 1*:

(A) *Biased-MF* (Koren et al., 2009): Classical latent factor model (Eq. 3).

(B) *HIALF* (Zhang et al., 2019): The model considering the historical influence but not utilizing reviews. Our model is based on this model.

(C) *Simi-avg.*: As baseline method, we predict ratings without LF integration, that is, $\hat{r}_{u,i} = e^{\text{simi}}_{u,i}$.

In *Task 2*, we compared our proposed model with *HIALF*.

Evaluation metric: The root mean square error (RMSE) was used for performance evaluation. It was calculated as:

$$\text{RMSE} = \sqrt{\frac{1}{|\mathcal{S}|} \sum_{(u,i)\in\mathcal{S}} (r_{u,i} - \hat{r}_{u,i})^2}, \tag{11}$$

where $\mathcal{S}$ denotes the set of user-item pairs in the test set. $r_{u,i}$ and $\hat{r}_{u,i}$ denote the ground-truth and predicted ratings of item i by user u, respectively. Note that in the test set in *Task 2*, the historical influence term in Eq. 8 (and Eq. 4) is equal to 0. This is because the test data have no historical ratings or reviews. This is equivalent to the following:

$$\hat{r}_{u,i} = \mu + b_u + b_i + p_u^\top q_i, \tag{12}$$

where b_u, b_i, p_u, and q_i are the learned parameters of *HIALF* and the proposed model.

Model training: In *Task 1*, we split the dataset into test (the last 25 ratings), validation (the last 50-26 ratings), and training (the rest of ratings). We used a validation set to tune the hyperparameters, and performance evaluation was conducted on the test set. For all models, we used $l = 5$ for the number of dimensions of the user preference and item feature vectors. The learning rate was searched in [0.005, 0.01, 0.05 0.1] for each model. For *Biased-MF*, the regularization parameter was searched in [0.005, 0.01, 0.05, 0.1]. For *HIALF*, we searched for the best hyperparameters in the range described by Zhang et al. (2019). For our model, we first searched for w and k in [0.0, 1.0, 3.0, 5.0, 7.0, 9.0] and [5, 10, 30, 50, 100], respectively. Then, four regularization parameters were searched in [0.000001, 0.00001 0.0001, 0.001, 0.01, 0.1]. We tokenized the review-sentences, and removed stop-words using NLTK (Bird and Klein, 2009). Then, reviews were vectorized by LDA using gensim (Řehůřek and Sojka, 2010). We used 10 for the number of topics according to the results of McAuley and Leskovec (2013). The stochastic gradient descent algorithm was used for optimization.

In *Task 2*, the datasets were split into test (first rating of every item) and training (the rest of ratings). We trained the model with the hyperparameters tuned in *Task 1*.

Computational resource of AI Bridging Cloud Infrastructure (ABCI) provided by National Institute of Advanced Industrial Science and Technology (AIST) was used.

6.2 Results and Discussions

Effect of w and k: We focus on the hyperparameters w and k in Eq. 9. Figure 3 shows RMSE in the Books dataset at various w and k. Here, *Simi-avg.* was used. We can see that $w = 5.0$, and $k = 30$ are the best values. The RMSE tends to improve at $w > 0$ when $k \geq 30$, indicating that weighing with the similarity is effective. Weighing is not effective when $k = 5$ or 10, because all extracted reviews have high similarities at these values. Additionally, the RMSE degrades when $k \geq 50$. This is because if we extract historical reviews that are too large, there may be low-similarity reviews.

Results of rating prediction in Task1: Table 4 illustrates the results of the rating prediction. Our model outperforms almost all baseline models. Additionally, we confirm that integrating LF (Table 4 (D)) improves the RMSE over *Simi-avg.* (Table 4 (C)). In the Clothing dataset, *Simi-avg.* performs better than *Ours*. This is because the LF model is not effective for pseudo-users, and there is only one non-pseudo-user in the Clothing dataset. These results indicate that we succeeded in integrating LF and the historical influence model.

Note that *Ours* and *Simi-avg.* use review textual information of target users. Since user ratings and reviews are usually provided at the same time, recommender systems cannot use reviews to predict ratings in practical situations. Therefore, *Task 2* can be more suitable for practical evaluations.

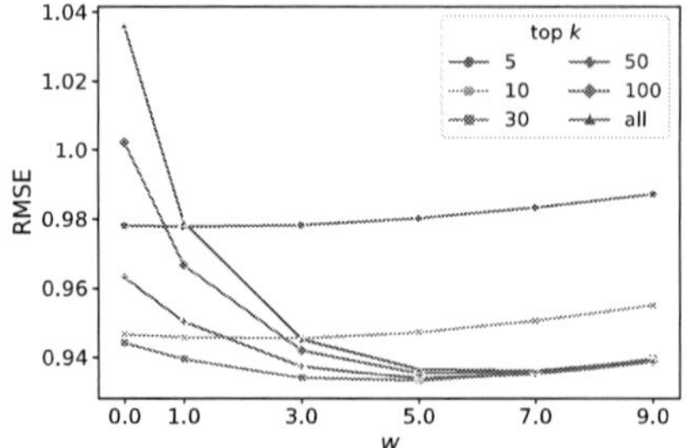

Figure 3: Effect of w and k. The y-axis represents RMSE, and x-axis represents w in Eq. 9. Each line represents k.

	Movies	Electronics	Clothing	Books
(A) *LF*	1.1002	1.4076	1.2061	1.0369
(B) *HIALF*	1.0644	1.3630	1.1739	1.0182
(C) *Simi-avg.*	1.0589	1.2015	**1.0789**	0.9332
(D) *Ours*	**1.0068**	**1.2001**	1.0800	**0.9261**
Ours vs *LF*	8.49%	14.74%	10.45%	10.68%
Ours vs *HIALF*	5.41%	11.95%	8.00%	9.04%

Table 4: Results of rating predictions (RMSE).

Results of intrinsic rating prediction in Task2: Table 5 shows the results of the intrinsic rating prediction. However, it is considered that the aspects of the pseudo-users are synthesized from many aspects of users. We consider that the RMSE calculated including the pseudo-user might contain noise. Thus, for a more personalized evaluation, we calculated RMSE without ratings of pseudo-users. In Table 5, the results show that our proposed model outperforms *HIALF* except for the Electronics dataset. This indicates that our model succeeds in separating historical influence and learning intrinsic preferences. Table 6 shows that our model has a better performance than *HIALF* in personalized evaluations. From these results, we consider that our model can predict the intrinsic ratings more accurately.

	Movies	Electronics	Clothing	Books
HIALF	1.0437	**1.2112**	1.0745	0.8971
Ours	**1.0302**	1.2118	**1.0673**	**0.8672**

Table 5: Results of predicting the first ratings. RMSE are reported in the table.

	Movies	Electronics	Clothing	Books
HIALF	1.0076	0.9222	(0.6886)	0.7388
Ours	**0.9959**	**0.8854**	**(0.6208)**	**0.7378**

Table 6: Results of predicting the first ratings **except for pseudo-users**. In the Clothing category, there is only one rating given by non-pseudo-user (reported in parentheses).

7 Conclusion

In this study, we propose an aspect-similarity-aware historical influence model for rating prediction. First, we perform preliminary experiments to validate our assumption that review aspects relate to the historical influence. From the analyses, we concluded that the sentence similarity relates to the historical influence. Thus, to model historical influence, we used textual information in user reviews, which previous models have ignored, for topic modeling. In the ordinay rating prediction task, we showed that the proposed approach achieved improvements over the previous historical-influence-aware models. Furthermore, to examine whether the proposed model can distinguish the intrinsic ratings of users from the historical influence, we conducted intrinsic rating prediction experiments. The results showed that our model has better performance than previous models.

Our method is limited to situations where the reviews of users are obtained before they provide ratings. For usual recommendation, it might not be practical. Thus, the method is not suitable for recommendations based on rating predictions. However, debiasing the historical influence to obtain intrinsic ratings can be considered as an application of our model. The intrinsic ratings would help subsequent users to make unbiased purchase decisions. In addition, recommender systems would be able to suggest acceptable items to users by using the intrinsic ratings. These improvements will provide better user experience of the e-commerce services.

References

Gediminas Adomavicius, Jesse Bockstedt, Shawn Curley, and Jingjing Zhang. 2016. Understanding Effects of Personalized vs. Aggregate Ratings on User Preferences. In *Proceedings of Joint Workshop on Interfaces and Human Decision Making for Recommender Systems*, IntRS '16, pages 14–21.

Rolph E. Anderson. 1973. Consumer Dissatisfaction: The Effect of Disconfirmed Expectancy on Perceived Product Performance. *Journal of Marketing Research*, 10(1):38–44.

Edward Loper Bird, Steven and Ewan Klein. 2009. Natural language processing with python.

David M. Blei, Andrew Y. Ng, and Michael I. Jordan. 2003. Latent dirichlet allocation. *J. Mach. Learn. Res.*, 3:993–1022.

Chong Chen, Min Zhang, Yiqun Liu, and Shaoping Ma. 2018. Neural Attentional Rating Regression with Review-level Explanations. In *Proceedings of the 2018 World Wide Web Conference*, WWW '18, pages 1583–1592.

Guibing Guo, Jie Zhang, Daniel Thalmann, Anirban Basu, and Neil Yorke-Smith. 2014. From Ratings to Trust: An Empirical Study of Implicit Trust in Recommender Systems. In *Proceedings of the 29th Annual ACM Symposium on Applied Computing*, SAC '14, pages 248–253.

Ruining He and Julian McAuley. 2016. Ups and Downs: Modeling the Visual Evolution of Fashion Trends with One-Class Collaborative Filtering. In *Proceedings of the 25th International Conference on World Wide Web*, WWW '16, pages 507–517.

Yehuda Koren, Robert Bell, and Chris Volinsky. 2009. Matrix Factorization Techniques for Recommender Systems. *Computer*, 42(8):30–37.

Munan Li, Kenji Tei, and Yoshiaki Fukazawa. 2019a. An efficient co-Attention Neural Network for Social Recommendation. In *IEEE/WIC/ACM International Conference on Web Intelligence*, WI '19, pages 34–42.

Pengfei Li, Hua Lu, Gang Zheng, Qian Zheng, Long Yang, and Gang Pan. 2019b. Exploiting Ratings, Reviews and Relationships for Item Recommendations in Topic Based Social Networks. In *Proceedings of the 2019 World Wide Web Conference*, WWW '19, pages 995–1005.

Guang Ling, Michael R. Lyu, and Irwin King. 2014. Ratings Meet Reviews, a Combined Approach to Recommend. In *Proceedings of the 8th ACM Conference on Recommender systems*, RecSys '14, pages 105–112.

Yiming Liu, Xuezhi Cao, and Yong Yu. 2016. Are You Influenced by Others When Rating?: Improve Rating Prediction by Conformity Modeling. In *Proceedings of the 10th ACM Conference on Recommender Systems*, RecSys '16, pages 269–272.

Julian McAuley and Jure Leskovec. 2013. Hidden Factors and Hidden Topics: Understanding Rating Dimensions with Review Text. In *Proceedings of the 7th ACM conference on Recommender systems*, RecSys '13, pages 165–172.

Subhabrata Mukherjee and Stephan Guennemann. 2019. GhostLink: Latent Network Inference for Influence-aware Recommendation. In *Proceedings of the 2019 World Wide Web Conference*, WWW '19, pages 1310–1320.

Radim Řehůřek and Petr Sojka. 2010. Software Framework for Topic Modelling with Large Corpora. In *Proceedings of the LREC 2010 Workshop on New Challenges for NLP Frameworks*, pages 45–50, May.

Yunzhi Tan, Min Zhang, Yiqun Liu, and Shaoping Ma. 2016. Rating-Boosted Latent Topics: Understanding Users and Items with Ratings and Reviews. In *Proceedings of the Twenty-Fifth International Joint Conference on Artificial Intelligence*, IJCAI'16, pages 2640–2646, July.

Ting Wang, Dashun Wang, and Fei Wang. 2014. Quantifying Herding Effects in Crowd Wisdom. In *Proceedings of the 20th ACM SIGKDD International Conference on Knowledge Discovery and Data Mining*, KDD '14, pages 1087–1096.

Le Wu, Peijie Sun, Yanjie Fu, Richang Hong, Xiting Wang, and Meng Wang. 2019a. A Neural Influence Diffusion Model for Social Recommendation. In *Proceedings of the 42nd International ACM SIGIR Conference on Research and Development in Information Retrieval*, SIGIR '19, pages 235–244.

Qitian Wu, Hengrui Zhang, Xiaofeng Gao, Peng He, Paul Weng, Han Gao, and Guihai Chen. 2019b. Dual Graph Attention Networks for Deep Latent Representation of Multifaceted Social Effects in Recommender Systems. In *Proceedings of the 2019 World Wide Web Conference*, WWW '19, pages 2091–2102.

Mao Ye, Xingjie Liu, and Wang-Chien Lee. 2012. Exploring Social Influence for Recommendation - A Generative Model Approach. In *Proceedings of the 35th International ACM SIGIR Conference on Research and Development in Information Retrieval*, SIGIR '12, pages 671–680.

Xiaoying Zhang, Hong Xie, Junzhou Zhao, and John C. S. Lui. 2019. Understanding Assimilation-contrast Effects in Online Rating Systems: Modelling, Debiasing, and Applications. *ACM Trans. Inf. Syst.*, 38(1):2:1–2:25.

Lei Zheng, Vahid Noroozi, and Philip S. Yu. 2017. Joint Deep Modeling of Users and Items Using Reviews for Recommendation. In *Proceedings of the Tenth ACM International Conference on Web Search and Data Mining*, WSDM '17, pages 425–434.

Distinctive Slogan Generation with Reconstruction

Shotaro Misawa   Yasuhide Miura   Tomoki Taniguchi   Tomoko Ohkuma

Fuji Xerox Co., Ltd.
`{misawa.shotaro,yasuhide.miura,`
`taniguchi.tomoki,ohkuma.tomoko}@fujixerox.co.jp`

Abstract

E-commerce sites include advertising slogans along with information regarding items. Slogans can attract viewers' attention to increase sales or visits by emphasizing advantages of items. The aim of this study is to generate a slogan from a description of an item. To generate a slogan, we apply an encoder–decoder model which has shown effectiveness in many kinds of natural language generation tasks, such as abstractive summarization. However, slogan generation task has three characteristics that distinguish it from other natural language generation tasks: distinctiveness, topic emphasis, and style difference. To handle these three characteristics, we propose a compressed representation–based reconstruction model with refer–attention and conversion layers. The results of experiments with automatic and human evaluations indicate that our method achieves higher performance than conventional methods.

1   Introduction

Advertisements, e-commerce sites, and flyers include advertising slogans along with item information, such as descriptions, prices, features, and pictures. Although the purpose of item information is to tell accurate and detailed information, the aim of slogans is to attract viewers' attention to increase sales or visits. Therefore, a slogan often emphasizes a part of advantages that an item holds, and it often contains peculiar words or expression to draw viewers' attention.

Creating slogans is cumbersome and costly. We propose a method to generate a slogan from a description of a target item to support the writers of slogans. Figure 1 shows an example of a description and a slogan for a job matching. A slogan is similar to an abstractive summary to some extent; a target sentence is shorter than a description and includes words not presented in the description. However, to attract viewers, slogans should have three unique characteristics. **Distinctiveness**: A slogan should be distinctive towards the target item. When a slogan is generic and suitable also for any other items, it does not increase the viewer's motivation to select the target item. Therefore, a slogan should describe the detail of a target-item. For example, "Don't go with the flow, but make a new flow by developing business social media" is better than "Why don't you apply to our company? We need you right now!" because the former provides more information regarding the job. **Topic Emphasis**: A slogan should examine a specific topic in the description because it is difficult to contain all aspects within a short tip. In fact, the example slogan in Figure 1 does not include phrases such as "business social media," which is one of the main topics in the description. **Style Difference**: A slogan should be written in an impressive writing style to attract viewers' interests. Therefore, a slogan differs from a description in terms of style and vocabulary. For instance, the first sentence of the example slogan is not just an explanation but an interrogative sentence.

To generate a slogan, we apply an encoder–decoder model (Bahdanau et al., 2014) since encoder–decoder models have shown effectiveness in abstractive summarization, and slogan generation shares some characteristics with abstractive summarization. However, slogan generation has three characteristics that differentiate it from abstractive summarization: distinctiveness, topic emphasis, and style difference. In particular, summarization models lose distinctiveness because their outputs tend to be generic (Gimpel et al., 2013).

Proceedings of the Workshop on Natural Language Processing in E-Commerce (EComNLP), pages 87–97
Barcelona, Spain (Online), Dec 12, 2020.

Figure 1 box:

> [Slogan]   How many times will you turn? We want marketers who will turn a PDCA-cycle at very high rate.
>
> [Description]
> We want to recruit marketing staffs for Wantedly. There are various products associated with the largest business social media, "*Wantedly*". Till date, we have registered with approximately 20,000 companies. We have developed a service that leads to "excitement at work" with the vision "We will be the infrastructure of all businesspeople in 2020!". To achieve that vision, we must operate a larger business at a higher speed than it currently is. We have many tasks for developing services. Will you join us to enhance the workplace for the future? Through work, you will turn a PDCA-cycle in a short period and maximize its effects! You cannot proceed if you don't try anything. Try "Code Wins Arguments," and scale new heights with *Wantedly*!
>
> Business contents: KPI design and management. / Making hypotheses and plans based on analysis data. / Planning and implementation of promotion. / Advertisement operation. / Writing of recruitment. / Nurturing and lead generation by MA tools. / Improving services based on hearing to customers.
>
> Graduates, people with programming experienced, and marketers who like new things are welcome. I would be glad to speak with you. Why not try new challenges with your colleagues and make a serious attempt at accomplishing something?

Figure 1: Example of a description and a slogan for a job-matching. Japanese–English translation.

To enhance distinctiveness, we define a reconstruction loss by introducing a reconstruction model that estimates the corresponding description from a slogan. The loss encourages the generation model to generate a distinctive slogan to help the estimation of the description. Here, slogan generation is a novel task in which information of a slogan is not equivalent to that of the description because of topic emphasis and style difference. Therefore, our reconstruction model generates a compressed representation of a description instead of the entire description. To ensure topic emphasis, we include a refer-attention layer that focuses on the partial description emphasized by a generated slogan into our model. To address style difference, we introduce a conversion layer that absorbs the style and vocabulary gaps between descriptions and slogans. We refer to this reconstruction model as a compressed representation–based reconstruction model (CRR).

The main contributions of our study can be summarized as follows.

- Propose a method that includes a compressed representation–based reconstruction model to generate distinctive slogans.

- Introduce the refer–attention and conversion layers for CRR to address topic emphasis and style difference, respectively.

- Evaluate the method using automatic and human evaluations.

- Compare the performance of non-neural and neural methods.

2   Related Work

Slogan Generation: Slogan generation has been addressed through non–neural approaches. One approach is to extract and revise a sentence from a corpus (Indrakanti et al., 2018; Iwama and Kano, 2018). Another approach is to construct skeletons of slogans and fill arbitrary words into the skeletons (Özbal et al., 2013; Alnajjar and Toivonen, 2020). In one study, suggestions for rephrasing written slogans were provided to assist slogan writers (Clark et al., 2018). Some approaches use a description of a target item (Žnidaršič et al., 2015; Chandler and Neupane, 2018), similarly to our method. These approaches consist from three steps: selecting slogans from a corpus as candidates, rephrasing candidate slogans, and sorting these slogans. However, the generated slogans are not creative because these methods essentially rephrase existing slogans. In contrast, our method is a neural–based generation model that generates slogans that are different from those in a corpus. The comparison of creativity between our method and a non-neural method is described in Section 5.3, in addition to the generation performance.

Abstractive Summarization: Summarization has been tackled by extractive and rule-based approaches (Vanderwende et al., 2007; Nenkova and McKeown, 2011; Nallapati et al., 2016a). However, neural based abstractive approaches have become very common and achieved high performance because of

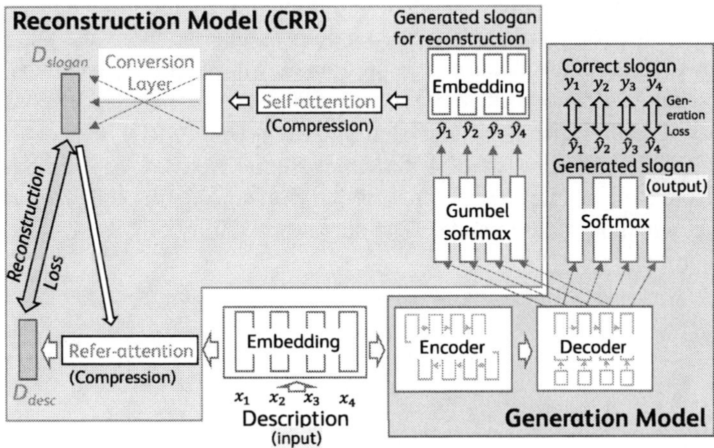

Figure 2: Outline of our method.

emerging large-scale datasets (Hermann et al., 2015) and powerful methods (Rush et al., 2015; Nallapati et al., 2016b; See et al., 2017) which are mainly based on an encoder–decoder model (Bahdanau et al., 2014). Because abstractive summarization is similar to slogan generation, neural abstractive methods will likely to improve the performance of slogan generation. On the other hand, these methods do not guarantee distinctiveness, topic emphasis, and style difference of generated texts which are required in slogans to improve sales or visits.

Reconstruction Model: Methods that include a reconstruction process have been proposed for text generation tasks. These methods combine a reconstruction model that generates a source sentence from information regarding a generated sentence, such as decoder's hidden states. Reconstruction models are used to improve the performance for low-resource data (Cheng et al., 2016) or application to monolingual data (Edunov et al., 2018) or multi-modal data (Delbrouck and Dupont, 2019). Some studies have introduced gumbel softmax (Niu et al., 2019) or reinforcement learning (Wang and Lee, 2018) to sample a generated sentence similar to our method. In addition, there is an approach to reconstruct the decoder's hidden states in video captioning (Wang et al., 2018). These methods reconstruct entire input sequences. However, this approach is inappropriate for slogan generation because of topic emphasis and style differences, thereby making a model difficult to reconstruct the entire description from a generated slogan. Our reconstruction model only generates a compressed representation, not a sentence or sequence, and the model includes mechanisms to ensure certain slogan characteristics.

3 Distinctive Slogan Generation with Reconstruction

A slogan should reflect a distinctive and important part of an item description. The more distinctive a slogan is, the easier the reconstruction of the corresponding description from the slogan is. This is because such slogans facilitate the estimation of the description. For example, the estimation of the corresponding description from the slogan "We need new staffs!" is difficult because it can fit to any other job. To enhance the distinctiveness of generated slogans, we define and minimize a reconstruction loss as an indicator of distinctiveness by introducing a compressed representation–based reconstruction model. To encourage topic emphasis and style difference, refer–attention and conversion layers are used, respectively. Figure 2 shows the outline of our method.

3.1 Generation Model

As a base generation model, any type of text generation models with an encoder–decoder model (Sutskever et al., 2014) can be applied. In our experiments, we employed two major approaches; an attentional encoder–decoder model (Bahdanau et al., 2014) and that with a copying mechanism (See et al., 2017). As training data, the base model requires pairs of a description and a correct slogan, and it is trained to generate the correct slogan from an input description.

Attentional Encoder-Decoder Model: Firstly, it divides a description into words. Secondly, it gets the embeddings of the description words. Here, we randomly initialize the embeddings and update these during training, however the embeddings can be pretrained. Thirdly, the embeddings are fed one-by-one into an encoder to calculate the context vector of the description. The encoder consists of a Recurrent Neural Network based model; specifically, a Gated Recurrent Unit (GRU) (Cho et al., 2014) is used.

Then, a decoder, which also consists of a Recurrent Neural Network based model, generates words from the context vector. It generates a word one-by-one with considering the previously generated word and the hidden representation of the decoder. The output probability of t-th word in a slogan, $P(\hat{w}_t)$, is calculable by equation 1.

$$P(\hat{w}_t) = \text{softmax}(W_G[h_t^G, C_t] + b_G) \tag{1}$$

$$h_t^G = \text{gru}(E(\hat{w}_{t-1}), h_{t-1}^G) \tag{2}$$

$$h_0^G = \tanh(W_0 ctx_I + b_0) \tag{3}$$

$$C_t = \sum_{i=1}^{I} a_i^t \cdot ctx_i \tag{4}$$

$$a_i^t = \text{softmax}(v \cdot \tanh(W_{att1} ctx_i + W_{att2} h_t^G + b_{att})) \tag{5}$$

where W_*, b_*, and v are trainable parameters, $[\cdot, \cdot]$ signifies the concatenation operation, $\hat{w}_t$ represents the t-th word of the predicted slogan, ctx_i denotes the context vector of the i-th word of the description, I is the length of the description, and $E(\cdot)$ signifies the embedding layer. In addition, softmax, tanh, and gru is a softmax, tangent hyperbolic, GRU function, respectively. The GRU function calculates the hidden states h_*^G from the previous hidden state of GRU and the previous word. During training, it uses the correct slogan word for $\hat{w}_{t-1}$ in equation 2. During inference, it uses beam search to find the best sentence.

Copying Mechanism: The decoder of an attentional encoder-decoder model is able to only generate words that exist in a predefined word vocabulary. To generate out-of-vocabulary words, this mechanism copies a word in an input description. Specifically, the probability of copying the words in a description follows the attention distribution in equation 5. That is, the word output probability is calculated from not only equation 1 but also from the attention distribution in equation 5. In addition, to balance these probabilities, it applies a parameter p_{gen}. Equations 6 and 7 show the calculation of the output probability of the t-th word in a slogan, $P_{copy}(\hat{w}_t)$.

$$P_{copy}(\hat{w}_t = w) = p_{gen}^t P(\hat{w}_t = w) + (1 - p_{gen}^t) \sum_{i:x_i=w} a_i^t \tag{6}$$

$$p_{gen}^t = \sigma(W_{pt1} ctx_* + W_{pt2} h_t + W_{pt3} E(\hat{w}_{t-1}) + b_{pt}) \tag{7}$$

where σ represents the sigmoid function, and x_i denotes the i-th word of a description.

3.2 Reconstruction Model with Refer-Attention and Conversion Layer

The reconstruction model is used to estimate the description from a generated slogan. To handle information inequivalence between descriptions and slogans, the model compresses a description and a generated slogan into representations, respectively. The reconstruction loss is calculated as the difference between the representation of a generated slogan (D_{slogan}) and that of a description (D_{desc}).

Generated Slogan Representation (D_{slogan}): The representation of a generated slogan can be obtained with word embeddings, but the standard generation process, such as beam search, is not differentiable. Therefore, we apply a gumbel–softmax layer (Jang et al., 2017) for which the input is the output from the generation model decoder (e.g. the output from equation 1). Equation 8 represents the process of sampling a slogan.

$$ss_t = gumbel(d_t) \tag{8}$$

where ss_t represents the t-th word of a sampled slogan, d_t signifies the decoder output of the t-th word, and $gumbel$ denotes the gumbel–softmax layer.

Then, the generated slogan representation is calculated from a weighted average of the word embeddings of the generated slogan which is sampled in equation 8. Here, slogans often contain words aiming at attracting notice and having no specific meaning, and these words are unnecessary for a reconstruction. Therefore, the words in slogans are weighted through the self–attention layer α_t^{self} inspired by the previous work (Vaswani et al., 2017) to ignore unnecessary words. The weighted representation Rep_{slogan} is calculated by equation 9.

$$Rep_{slogan} = \sum_{t=1}^{T} \alpha_t^{self} E(ss_t) \tag{9}$$

$$\alpha_t^{self} = \frac{\exp(att_{base}^t)}{\sum_{j=1}^{T} \exp(att_{base}^j)} \tag{10}$$

$$att_{base}^t = W_{a1}(\tanh(W_{a2}\{E(ss_t) + b_{a2}\}) + b_{a1} \tag{11}$$

where T signifies the length of a generated slogan.

There is style difference between slogans and descriptions, such as word usage or writing style. To learn and adjust style difference, a conversion layer is applied. Equation 12 shows the representation of a generated slogan with this conversion layer.

$$D_{slogan} = W_c(Rep_{slogan}) + b_c \tag{12}$$

Description Representation (D_{desc}): The representation of a description is defined by a weighted average of the word embeddings of the words in a description. Here, a slogan pays attention to a specific part of the description because of topic emphasis. Therefore, we introduce the refer–attention layer α_i^{refer} to examine specific description words that a generated slogan emphasizes. The description representation D_{desc} is calculable by equation 13.

$$D_{desc} = \sum_{i=1}^{I} \alpha_i^{refer} \times E(x_i) \tag{13}$$

Since the refer–attention layer should be able to find parts which a generated slogan focused on, α_i^{refer} should be calculated by considering both the slogan representation D_{source} and a word in the description. Equation 14 presents the calculation of the refer attention for the i-th word of a description.

$$\alpha_i^{refer} = \frac{\exp(v_r u_i)}{\sum_{j=1}^{I} \exp(v_r u_j)} \tag{14}$$

$$u_i = \tanh(W_{r1} D_{slogan} + W_{r2} E(x_i) + b_r) \tag{15}$$

where v_r signifies the trainable parameter.

3.3 Objective Function

To optimize the generation and reconstruction models, we define generation and reconstruction losses, respectively. When training the both models, we optimize the total loss that is combined loss of the generation and reconstruction losses. When combining, it multiplies λ by the reconstruction loss to balances these losses. Equation 16 shows the total loss L.

$$L = L_1 + \lambda \times L_2 \tag{16}$$

Generation Loss: The generation loss is defined as the cross-entropy loss between generated and correct slogans. Equation 17 shows the generation loss L_1.

$$L_1 = -\sum_{k=1}^{K} \log \hat{c}_k \tag{17}$$

	Train	Dev.	Test
# pairs of a description and a slogan	58,461	6,290	7,573
avg. slogan length	15.59	15.38	15.57
avg. description length	347.14	314.75	362.67

Table 1: Data specifications

Dataset	uni-gram	tri-gram
Abstractive Summary	68.4%	17.3%
Slogan	63.0%	8.7%

Table 2: The average rate of a target sentence uni- and tri-grams that exist in the corresponding source sentence

where K signifies the length of a correct slogan and $\hat{c}_k$ represents the generation probability of the k-th word of the correct slogan.

Reconstruction Loss: The reconstruction loss should become lower when D_{desc} and D_{slogan} are similar. In our experiment, the reconstruction loss is defined by using the cosine similarity between the representations of generated and correct slogans. Equation 18 shows the reconstruction loss L_2.

$$L_2 = 1 - cos(D_{desc}, D_{slogan}) \tag{18}$$

where $cos(D_{desc}, D_{slogan})$ represents the cosine similarity between D_{desc} and D_{slogan}.

4 Experimental Settings

4.1 Dataset

We used a dataset collected from *Wantedly*[1], a Japanese job matching website. The data includes many pairs of slogans and descriptions, which is a requirement of this study. The descriptions include job details and requirements.

Each job has the corresponding company, and each company has 10.2 jobs on average. Slogans of the same company tend to become similar to each other. Therefore, data were split into three sets with the ratio of 8 : 1 : 1, provided that the data of the same company belong to the same set. Table 1 presents the data specifications.

We compared this slogan dataset with a Japanese newspaper corpus of abstractive summary [2]. Table 2 represents the rate of a target sentence (e.g. slogan) uni-gram and tri-gram that appear in the source sentence (e.g. description). By comparing abstractive summaries and slogans, slogans contain more words that do not appear in the source sentence. Furthermore, tri-grams of slogans are more unseen in the source sentence than that of summaries. These results indicate that the writing style of slogans is different from that of descriptions, thus making slogan generation more difficult than abstractive summarization.

4.2 Comparison Methods

Non-neural Method: As a non–neural method, we developed Case–based slogan production (Žnidaršič et al., 2015) (Case–Base). It retrieves a relevant case from training data and rewrites some words by considering part of speech tags.

Neural Baseline Methods: As neural baselines, we prepared an attentional encoder–decoder (EncDec) model and that with a copying mechanism (Copy).

Conventional Method of Reconstruction: To compare our method with the method of reconstructing an entire sentence, we developed a method in which the reconstruction model generates a full description from a slogan by introducing an EncDec model (Niu et al., 2019) (EncDec+RecText).

Proposed Methods: We prepared our methods with the generation model of EncDec (EncDec+CRR) and Copy (Copy+CRR).

Other Configurations of Proposed Method: To investigate the effect of the attention layer in CRR, we replaced the refer–attention layer with an average pooling layer (EncDec+CRR-woAtt). To examine the effect of the conversion layer, we developed a CRR without the conversion layer (EncDec+CRR-woConv).

---

[1]https://www.wantedly.com
[2]https://mainichi.jp/contents/edu/03.html

	ROUGE-L
Case-Base (Žnidaršič et al., 2015)	13.41
EncDec (Bahdanau et al., 2014)	16.77
EncDec+RecText (Niu et al., 2019)	17.14
EncDec+CRR-woAtt	17.61
EncDec+CRR-woConv	17.89
EncDec+CRR	**18.10**
Copy (See et al., 2017)	18.50
Copy+CRR	**19.38**

Table 3: Automatic evaluation results. Bold indicates the best score for each baseline.

	Distinc.	Adeq.	Flu.
Copy	47.5	49.8	50.0
Copy+CRR	**52.5**	**50.2**	50.0

Table 4: Human evaluation results. Bold indicates the best score for each measure.

4.3 Configurations

Data Preprocess: We used NEologd (Sato et al., 2017) for word segmentation. We removed non-frequent words which was over 50,000 words in frequent order.

Hyperparameters: We run five experiments for each parameter and selected λ and p which achieved the best ROUGE-L performance for the development data. λ was selected from $\{0.5, 1.0, 2.0, 3.0, 4.0, 5.0\}$. The value of λ was set to 4.0 with the performance of EncDec+CRR. The value of p was set to 0.6 from $\{0.1, 0.2, 0.3, \cdots, 0.8, 0.9, 1.0\}$. The other parameters were decided by the performance of EncDec. The dimensions of embeddings and GRU were 200. In addition, Adam optimizer with the default parameter of pytorch was used for optimization, and the beam size of inference was 5.

4.4 Evaluation Metrics

Automatic Evaluation: We run 10 experiments and used the average of ROUGE-L (Lin, 2004) which is a popular metric of language generation tasks. ROUGE-L is the longest common sequence-based statics. We calculated ROUGE score using the public python script of rouge [3] (version 0.3.0).

Human Evaluation: We conducted a pairwise comparison of Copy and Copy+CRR via crowdsourcing. Both methods generated slogans for 250 randomly sampled descriptions from the test data. Each worker judges the generated slogans in terms of distinctiveness (Distinc.), adequacy (Adeq.), and fluency (Flu.) by looking at a description of a target job and slogans generated by Copy and Copy+CRR. We took the majority vote of evaluations of 10 workers. Distinctiveness is a measure of how specialized a slogan is to the corresponding description. Adequacy is that of how faithful a slogan is to the description. Fluency refers to how natural a slogan is.

5 Results and Discussion

5.1 Automatic Evaluation Result

Table 3 presents the automatic evaluation results. Note that slogans are creative, therefore the ROUGE-L performance itself is relatively lower than other tasks.

Non-neural method vs Neural methods: The results indicate that all of the neural methods outperform Case-Base which is the non–neural conventional method. Moreover, the performance gap between non-neural and neural methods was quite large.

Baseline method vs Proposed method: When comparing EncDec with EncDec+CRR and Copy with Copy+CRR, the methods with CRR outperformed its baseline method. This result indicates that our reconstruction model improves the performance of slogan generation.

RecText vs CRR: EncDec+RecText also achieved higher performance than EncDec; however, its performance was worse than that of EncDec+CRR. This result suggests that reconstructing the entire description is inappropriate for slogan generation. Here, we observed that the descriptions reconstructed

---

[3]https://github.com/pltrdy/rouge

Methods	Slogan
Correct	How many times will you turn? We want a marketer who will turn a PDCA-cycle at very high rate.
Copy	We want a person who will be in charge of marketing of the future!
Copy+CRR	We want a marketer who will make a new service at the speed of light!

Table 5: Example outputs. The description is presented in Figure 1.

Methods	Creativity
Case-Base	59.67
Copy+CRR	69.81

Methods	Distinctiveness
Copy	75.34
Copy+CRR	71.27

Table 6: Creativity comparison between non-neural and neural methods

Table 7: Distinctiveness comparison between baseline and our methods

by RecText were quite poor. We have concluded that the reconstruction loss in RecText tends to focus on generating a fluent description than enhancing the distinctiveness of a slogan.

Effect of Each Component of CRR: Both the refer–attention and conversion layers also had positive effects when comparing CRR, CRR-woAtt, and CRR-woConv. In particular, the effect of the refer–attention layer was greater than that of the conversion layer. One reason for this may be that style difference is absorbed by not only the conversion layer but also the self–attention layer.

5.2 Human Evaluation Result

Table 4 presents the results of the human evaluation. Our method performed better in terms of distinctiveness; this illustrates that CRR is effective in reflecting distinctive information of a description. Adequacy of Copy+CRR was slight better than that of Copy; it represents that our method can capture correct information of the target job even though generic slogans (i.e. less distinctiveness) have less risk of containing wrong information. In terms of Fluency, the two methods were equal. It indicates that CRR does not adversely affect the language modeling of the generation model.

5.3 Discussion

Example Outputs: Table 5 presents the correct slogan and outputs from Copy and Copy+CRR of which descriptions are presented in Figure 1. The output from Copy includes "marketing" as a word related to the description. The output from Copy+CRR includes "speed of light" in addition to "marketer"; it indicates that our method can describe more distinctive information of a description. Moreover, "speed of light" is a metaphor and does not naturally appear in a job description. Such expression in slogans might draw attention of readers. In terms of drawing attention, the generated slogan of Copy+CRR seems better than the expression "at very high rate" in the correct slogan. This might be because the generation model prefers extreme words or phrases to make it easier to distinguish the target job from another job. However, it is still difficult to generate the first sentence of the correct slogan.

Creativity of Neural Method: To confirm that neural methods can generate more creative slogans than non-neural methods, we measured creativity of the slogans generated by Case-Base and Copy+CRR. Here, we define creativity as the similarity of the generated slogans and the training data. We measured ROUGE-L between a generated slogan and the slogan that is most similar to the generated slogan in the training data. Table 6 represents the average score of Case-Base and Copy+CRR. The result indicates that our neural method is more creative than the conventional non–neural method.

Distinctiveness of Outputs: To verify that our method can generate more distinctive slogans than a conventional method, we calculated distinctiveness of the generated slogans. As an alternative measure of distinctiveness, we assessed the similarity of the slogans generated for the target job and another job. This is because the generated slogans become dissimilar when each slogan is distinctive towards the target job, given that each job is different each other. We calculated the averaged ROUGE-L between each generated slogan and the most similar generated slogan in the test data. Table 7 illustrates the score

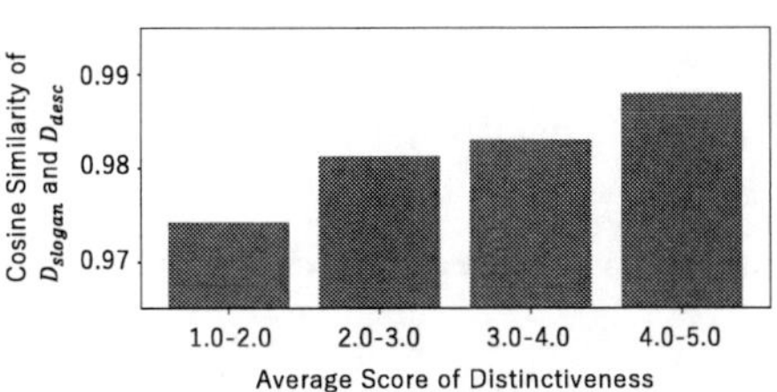

Figure 3: Relationship between distinctiveness and cosine similarity of representations

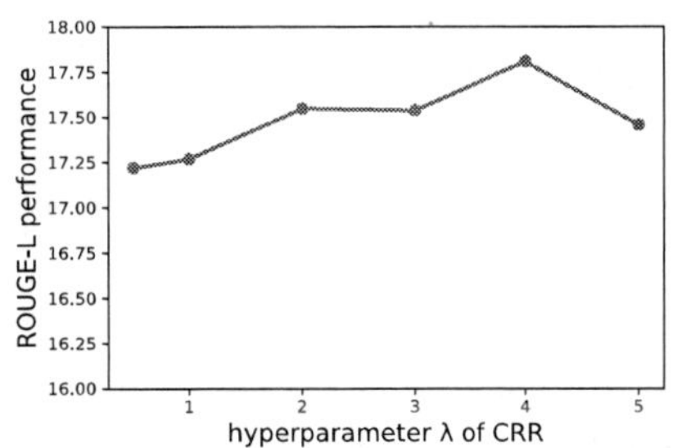

Figure 4: Performance curve of different λ of EncDec+CRR

of Copy and Copy+CRR. The result suggests that the outputs from Copy+CRR are more dissimilar from each other than the outputs from Copy. Therefore, CRR induces distinctiveness in the generated slogans.

Effect of Reconstruction Model: By updating the reconstruction model, the reconstruction loss could be reduced. To check whether the generation model changes output tips to reduce the reconstruction loss, we evaluated the reconstruction loss when the loss is backpropagate to only the reconstruction model (OnlyR) and to the both reconstruction and generation models (Both). That is, OnlyR was trained to estimate the description from the generated slogan which is an intact output from the generation model. The reconstruction loss for Both was 0.006, however that for OnlyR was 0.112. This result indicates that the reconstruction loss makes the generation model generate slogans which can be a clue to the estimation of the description.

To authorize the assumption that the reconstruction is easy when generated slogans are distinctive, we compared distinctiveness of generated slogans and the ease of the reconstruction of the description from a slogan. As a measure of distinctiveness, workers in human evaluation evaluated 250 slogans generated by Copy+CRR in terms of distinctiveness on a scale from 1 to 5. As a measure of the ease of the reconstruction, we used $cos(D_{desc}, D_{slogan})$ in the reconstruction loss when generating the slogan. Figure 3 presents the relationship between the averaged distinctiveness scores and the cosine similarities. This result suggests that the generated slogan becomes distinctive as it can estimate the description of the target job accurately. That is, it supports our assumption that the difficulty of reconstruction is related to the distinctiveness of generated slogans.

Effect of Hyperparameter λ: To analyze the effect of λ, we examined the relationship between the performance and λ. Figure 4 shows the performance curve of different λ. The figure shows that the best λ is 4.0. However, the variation in the performance for λ is relatively small. It indicates that the parameter λ is not sensitive, and our method does not hurt the performance if choosing wrong λ.

Note that the best λ is over 1.0, therefore the method seems to emphasize L_2 in equation 16. However, the value of the reconstruction loss is very small, and the method mainly focuses on the generation loss while referring to the reconstruction loss.

6 Conclusion

The aim of this study is to generate a slogan from the description of a target item. We firstly apply an encoder–decoder model to the slogan generation task. Then, we focus on the three characteristics of slogan generation: distinctiveness, topic emphasis, style difference. To enhance the distinctiveness of generated slogans, we define and minimize a reconstruction loss as an indicator of distinctiveness by introducing a compressed representation–based reconstruction model. To encourage topic emphasis and style difference, refer–attention and conversion layers are used, respectively. Automatic and human evaluation demonstrated that our method is superior to the conventional methods. In addition, we observed that neural methods are superior to a non-neural method in terms of ROUGE-L performance and creativity. In future work, we are planning to make a generation model which can directly enhance sales or visits by optimizing more straightforward e-commerce signals. Moreover, we will like to conduct an experiment with another dataset to ensure the generalizability of our method.

References

Khalid Alnajjar and Hannu Toivonen. 2020. Computational generation of slogans. *Natural Language Engineering*, pages 1–33.

Dzmitry Bahdanau, Kyunghyun Cho, and Yoshua Bengio. 2014. Neural machine translation by jointly learning to align and translate. *arXiv preprint arXiv:1409.0473*.

Bryant Chandler and Aadesh Neupane. 2018. Slogatron: Advanced wealthiness generator. *arXiv preprint arXiv:1809.09563*.

Yong Cheng, Wei Xu, Zhongjun He, Wei He, Hua Wu, Maosong Sun, and Yang Liu. 2016. Semi-supervised learning for neural machine translation. In *Proceedings of the 54th Annual Meeting of the Association for Computational Linguistics (Volume 1: Long Papers)*, pages 1965–1974.

Kyunghyun Cho, Bart van Merrienboer, Dzmitry Bahdanau, and Yoshua Bengio. 2014. On the properties of neural machine translation: Encoder-decoder approaches. In *Eight Workshop on Syntax, Semantics and Structure in Statistical Translation*.

Elizabeth Clark, Anne S. Ross, Chenhao Tan, Yangfeng Ji, and Noah A. Smith. 2018. Creative writing with a machine in the loop: Case studies on slogans and stories. In *Proceedings of the 23rd International Conference on Intelligent User Interfaces*, pages 329–340.

Jean-Benoit Delbrouck and Stephane Dupont. 2019. Adversarial reconstruction for multi-modal machine translation. *arXiv preprint arXiv:1910.02766*.

Sergey Edunov, Myle Ott, Michael Auli, and David Grangier. 2018. Understanding back-translation at scale. In *Proceedings of the 2018 Conference on Empirical Methods in Natural Language Processing*, pages 489–500.

Kevin Gimpel, Dhruv Batra, Chris Dyer, and Gregory Shakhanarovich. 2013. A systematic exploration of diversity in machine translation. In *Proceedings of the 2013 Conference on Empirical Methods in Natural Language Processing*, pages 1100–1111.

Karl Moritz Hermann, Tomáš Kočiský, Edward Grefenstette, Lasse Espeholt, Will Kay, Mustafa Suleyman, and Phil Blunsom. 2015. Teaching machines to read and comprehend. In *Proceedings of the 28th International Conference on Neural Information Processing Systems - Volume 1*, page 1693–1701.

Saratchandra Indrakanti, Gyant Singh, and Justin House. 2018. Blurb mining: Discovering interesting excerpts from e-commerce product reviews. In *Companion Proceedings of the The Web Conference 2018*, pages 1669–1675.

Kango Iwama and Yoshinobu Kano. 2018. Japanese advertising slogan generator using case frame and word vector. In *Proceedings of the 11th International Conference on Natural Language Generation*, pages 197–198.

Eric Jang, Shixiang Gu, and Ben Poole. 2017. Categorical reparameterization with gumbel-softmax. In *Proceedings of the International Conference on Learning Representations*.

Chin-Yew Lin. 2004. Rouge: A package for automatic evaluation of summaries. In *Proceedings of The Workshop on Text Summarization Branches Out at the 42nd Annual Meeting of the Association for Computational Linguistics*, pages 74–81.

Ramesh Nallapati, Feifei Zhai, and Bowen Zhou. 2016a. Summarunner: A recurrent neural network based sequence model for extractive summarization of documents. *arXiv preprint arXiv:1611.04230*.

Ramesh Nallapati, Bowen Zhou, Caglar Gulcehre, Bing Xiang, et al. 2016b. Abstractive text summarization using sequence-to-sequence rnns and beyond. *arXiv preprint arXiv:1602.06023*.

Ani Nenkova and Kathleen McKeown. 2011. *Automatic summarization*. Now Publishers Inc.

Xing Niu, Weijia Xu, and Marine Carpuat. 2019. Bi-directional differentiable input reconstruction for low-resource neural machine translation. In *Proceedings of the 2019 Conference of the North American Chapter of the Association for Computational Linguistics: Human Language Technologies, Volume 1 (Long and Short Papers)*, pages 442–448.

Gözde Özbal, Daniele Pighin, and Carlo Strapparava. 2013. Brainsup: Brainstorming support for creative sentence generation. In *Proceedings of the 51st Annual Meeting of the Association for Computational Linguistics (Volume 1: Long Papers)*, pages 1446–1455.

Alexander M. Rush, Sumit Chopra, and Jason Weston. 2015. A neural attention model for abstractive sentence summarization. In *Proceedings of the 2015 Conference on Empirical Methods in Natural Language Processing*, pages 379–389.

Toshinori Sato, Taiichi Hashimoto, and Manabu Okumura. 2017. Implementation of a word segmentation dictionary called mecab-ipadic-neologd and study on how to use it effectively for information retrieval (in japanese). In *Proceedings of the Twenty-three Annual Meeting of the Association for Natural Language Processing*, pages NLP2017–B6–1. The Association for Natural Language Processing.

Abigail See, Peter J. Liu, and Christopher D. Manning. 2017. Get to the point: Summarization with pointer-generator networks. In *Proceedings of the 55th Annual Meeting of the Association for Computational Linguistics (Volume 1: Long Papers)*, pages 1073–1083.

Ilya Sutskever, Oriol Vinyals, and Quoc V. Le. 2014. Sequence to sequence learning with neural networks. In *Proceedings of 2014 Conference on the Advances in neural information processing systems*, pages 3104–3112.

Martin Žnidaršič, Polona Tomašič, and Gregor Papa. 2015. Case-based slogan production. In *Proceedings of The Workshop on Experience and Creativity at the 23rd International Conference on Case-Based Reasoning*, pages 123–130.

Lucy Vanderwende, Hisami Suzuki, Chris Brockett, and Ani Nenkova. 2007. Beyond sumbasic: Task-focused summarization with sentence simplification and lexical expansion. *Information Processing & Management*, 43(6):1606–1618.

Ashish Vaswani, Noam Shazeer, Niki Parmar, Jakob Uszkoreit, Llion Jones, Aidan N.Gomez, Lukasz Kaiser, and Illia Polosukhin. 2017. Attention is all you need. In *Proceedings of the 31st Conference on Neural Information Processing Systems*.

Yaushian Wang and Hung-Yi Lee. 2018. Learning to encode text as human-readable summaries using generative adversarial networks. In *Proceedings of the 2018 Conference on Empirical Methods in Natural Language Processing*, pages 4187–4195.

Bairui Wang, Lin Ma, Wei Zhang, and Wei Liu. 2018. Reconstruction network for video captioning. In *Proceedings of the IEEE Conference on Computer Vision and Pattern Recognition*, pages 7622–7631.

Association for Computational Linguistics
209 N. Eighth Street
Stroudsburg, Pennsylvania 18360

ISBN 978-1-7138-2826-6